Finding the Way Again

Books by Michael Lister

For Kathy,
Behold the Man!
Best wishes & Blessing

Finding the Way Again

**Rediscovering Radical Love and Freedom
in the Lost Teachings of Jesus**

Michael Lister

11-25-11

Pulpwood Press

You buy a book. We plant a tree.

This book was made possible through the generosity of
Dr. David Lister
John Bridges
Mike and Judi Lister

Inquiries should be addressed to:
Pulpwood Press
P.O. Box 35038
Panama City, FL 32412

Lister, Michael.
Finding the Way Again / Michael
Lister.
-----1st ed.

p.   cm.
ISBN: 978-1-888146-81-3 (hardback)
ISBN: 978-1-888146-82-0 (trade paperback)
ISBN: 978-1-888146-83-7(ebook)

Library of Congress Control Number:

Book Design by Adam Ake

Printed in the United States

1 3 5 7 9 10 8 6 4 2

First Edition

For Ansley

Introduction

After dedicating this book to me, Michael honored me further by inviting me to write the introduction. I accepted, and have the privilege of inviting you into this lovely, inspiring, and challenging work.

Beyond the hymns, the stain glass, the pictures of a haloed Caucasian Jesus, and the over-emphasizing of his divinity at the expense of his humanity, there is a man, a fully human man who is also God in the flesh.

Perhaps if we would step out of our well-programmed paradigms we would see the fully human Jesus walking, laughing, weeping, and feeling—truly one of us. Why does it matter? Why should we go to the trouble and discomfort of looking at Jesus again? Because we've lost our way, we've lost *the* way.

Like Michelangelo chiseling David out of a cold, lifeless block of marble, we must extract Jesus from the wrong and rigid traditions, false idols, and layers and layers of misunderstanding and misinterpretation into which we have placed him. In doing so, the love, grace, and freedom that only Jesus of Nazareth can offer will become clear and attainable.

Over twenty years ago I came across a beautiful picture of Jesus, a media kit still from Franco Zeffirelli's miniseries *Jesus of Nazareth*, which I had framed and gave to Michael as a gift because of our mutual love of Jesus. For over two decades it has hung in every office he's had and even looked over him as he wrote the insightful entries contained in this book.

If you're like me, you'll wrestle at times with the radical Jesus Michael portrays. This is to be expected. If a portrait of Jesus doesn't challenge, and at times shock and scandalize us, in the same way he did those who first encountered him, we're not being presented with a very accurate picture of the man who was so unsettling he was believed to be deranged and demon possessed.

With Michael's work here, we have the opportunity to see with new eyes a clearer picture of Jesus, hear with new ears more of the true meaning of his message. All we need are hearts and minds that are open—as Jesus put it, eyes to see and ears to hear. It's my prayer that we will. And that it won't stop there, but in seeing and hearing we will accept the call to truly follow Jesus, changing our vision of God to his, making his priorities ours—living compassionately, caring for the poor and oppressed, feeding the hungry, loving enemies, blessing cursers, praying for users and abusers, and becoming like children again. If this sounds like something you want to join me in doing then turn the page and behold the man.

Ansley Henkel
Atlanta, GA
November, 2011

Preface

This is a work of restoration.

As if a conservator refurbishing an ancient mosaic in a pre-modern monastery, I am attempting to restore, repair, and preserve what I believe to be the truest, most accurate image of Jesus.

In no way meant to be comprehensive or exhaustive, this small, specific volume addresses what I feel has been lost, stolen, and obscured about Jesus—his message and the meaning of his life. If I lived in a different time and place this would be a different book.

From the very beginning, Jesus has been appropriated, his message altered—added to and taken away from—by culture, religion, his family and first followers, Paul, the Roman Empire, the Christian religion, and on and on, up until and, despite my best efforts, including, me. For even as I attempt to restore and reveal, I unwittingly alter and conceal. Thus, this is, inevitably, *my* gospel, *my* Jesus as much as anything else.

What I offer is not dogma or doctrine but discussion—a contribution to the ongoing conversation between open seekers of understanding and enlightenment. I write this as one asking questions far more than offering answers.

The concepts I share and the language I use to convey them are meant to inspire, not offend, to provoke thought not anger, and I hope you will receive them in that spirit. My intention is to be accurate and expressive, to place these timeless, transcendent truths in language that restores the original power, provocation, and profundity of Jesus and his message.

These essays, written over many years, represent over three decades of dedication and serious study, and are informed by the work of scholars in the field, but this is a devotional, not an academic book—personal reflections born out of my passion for Jesus, his vision, mission, and message.

Look closely.

Beneath the layers and layers of dust and dirt, of history and tradition, culture and religion, there is a more perfect picture awaiting rediscovery. Behind the cosmic Christ there is Jesus, an illegitimate peasant with the power of God on his tongue and in his hands. Beyond the icon, there is an iconoclast who overturns temple tables and kicks down fear-based religion and class-based divisions and proclaims God's unconditional love until it gets him killed. In some small way I hope my work here helps to uncover, restore, and preserve in the purest sense possible the authentic message of the man behind the man, the son of man who both is and shows the way.

Lost Gospel

The true way and good news of Jesus has been lost.
It's not an ancient manuscript or long lost papyrus awaiting discovery. Nor is it hidden inside one of the Gnostic gospels that claim to contain secrets Jesus only shared with a select few.

Like Poe's "Purloined Letter," the teachings of Jesus are hidden in plain view. They are not buried in a yet-to-be-discovered cave or veiled in secrecy for a few intellectual elites. They are calling to us across space and time, culture and language, their clarity and poignancy available for those who have ears to hear and eyes to see. All we have to do is behold the man and respond to his call to be truly free and compassionate.

There's a disconnect between Jesus and Christianity as a religion, the church as an institution, and those who claim to be his followers. We have lost our way—and we're not the first. From the very beginning, this man of mystery has been largely misunderstood by his followers, family members, and friends.

We've lost the way—the radical Jewish peasant who began a revolution so many years ago. We've mishandled Jesus's identity—we've clung to the easy divinity of the Christ of the church while ignoring the difficult humanity of Jesus of Nazareth. We've exchanged something beautiful for a bully pulpit, something brilliant for something blunt, something sublime for something silly, overly simplistic, often superfluous. We've replaced the gospel *of* Jesus with the gospel *about* Jesus. We've interpreted the life and teachings of Jesus in the light of the Bible and church history instead of interpreting the Bible and everything else in the light of the life and teachings of Jesus. We've domesticated and subverted his subversive stories, nationalized his universal message. We've turned his sweeping call for an uncompromising commitment to love into the dos and don'ts of moralism. We've largely ignored what he emphasized and overemphasized what he never mentioned. We've neglected, changed, betrayed, and denied his message—all the while constantly calling ourselves by his name.

We need a reminder of what matters most, of what is essential, of how we might clear away all the layers and silence all the voices so we can see and hear, and in seeing and hearing, be without excuse for not doing.

It's not too late to discover the lost gospel of Jesus and begin to live by it, to change our direction, to once again become people of the way. We could, with humility, embody compassion and justice. We could so completely trust God that we dare to share what we have with those in need, love those who hate us, bless those who curse us.

What's been lost can be found again. Do we dare? Can we hear the call clearly and be so moved we must respond? If we sense that something profound and precious has been lost, we can do something about it. It's like a treasure that's been lost, long since buried in a field. All we have to do is go and sell all we have and buy the field.

My goal with this intentionally simple, slim volume (based on scholarship, but not bogged down by notes and references) is to attempt to remove that which has obscured, hidden, and even replaced Jesus and his radical revolution, extricating him from the stiflingly narrow religious context that all but silences him, so his message can reverberate around us, resonate within us.

There is hope.

This can happen.

If Jesus teaches us anything, it is that which was once dead can live again, that which was lost can be found.

One Word

One word.

One little word to say it all.

If only one word of Jesus's had survived, one word to capture his essence, summarize his message, convey his meaning, explain his life, one word would be enough. All we would need is *abba*—one of the few words we actually have in Jesus's native language of Aramaic.

Abba is Aramaic for dad—not the formal father, but the intimate, informal daddy or papa. It's more akin to the airy dada softly spoken by an infant than the address of dad by an older child.

It's staggering—even now, so long after the concept was introduced: God, the author of creation, the designer of the universe, the ground of all being, invites us to be intimate with him.

Abba is the gospel in a single word. Like a drop of sea water containing all the elements of the ocean or an acorn encapsulating an enormous oak entire, abba captures Jesus's concept of the Kingdom of God.

According to Jesus, God is not angry or aloof, awaiting appeasement, but our daddy who adores us, a papa who wants to lavish his love upon us if only we will let him.

God is not a severe cosmic judge anxious to inflict punishment, but a loving, kind, gentle, and strong dad. All you have to do is look at the birds of the air, Jesus says, they don't sow or reap or store away in barns, yet our heavenly father feeds them. Are you not much more valuable than they? Your heavenly daddy knows what you need even before you ask him.

Think of a good dad (even if you didn't have one, you'll likely know of one). That's all you need to do to understand God. Which one of you, if your son asks for bread, will give him a stone? Or if he asks for a fish, will give him a snake? If you, then, though you are evil know how to give good gifts to your children, how much more will your abba in heaven give good gifts to those who ask him?

Jesus didn't just call God Abba, didn't just communicate that's who God is, he demonstrated it. Jesus embodied closeness, connection, intimacy with God. His knowledge that God was his father informed everything he said and did. Everyone sensed it. This man was different; his connection to God was different. When he taught, the people were amazed. He spoke with authority. His boldness and absolute certainty in God's love were based on his experience of it. He trusted God, and it showed—and he knew that if we could only trust God's love, too, our deepest needs and most intense longings would be satisfied.

Jesus lived in the light of Dad's love, and it shone on his face, burned in his eyes. He was intimate, the epitome of being one. His entire existence was centered in Dad. He did Dad's will.

Perhaps more than in any other area of his life, Jesus's prayers showed us what our relationship with our dad can be like. He'd rise early every morning to start his day with Dad, and ended it the same way, often praying through the night.

One prayer of Jesus's is particularly revealing. It took place on the night of his arrest. More than any other, this plea/prayer conveyed the warmth, intimacy, and dependency that was the norm of his experiences. It was during this time, aware of what was about to happen, his disciples having abandoned him for sleep, that Jesus's true relationship with his abba shown through. His prayer was that of a small child: Daddy, Daddy, please don't make me drink this bitter cup. Please, Daddy, let it pass from me. Don't make me. Nevertheless, I trust you. Not my will, but yours be done.

Of course, Jesus's quintessential teaching on the fatherhood of God is embodied in his parable that is often referred to as the parable of the prodigal son. It'd be more accurate to call it the parable of the patient father, for it shows us his deep concern and unconditional love for both of his sons.

God, the parable reveals, is like a father who even after his children break his heart and reject him, still loves us. Not only does he love us, but he is willing to welcome us home any time we are willing to return. In fact, he will rise and run toward us at the first hint of our return. He loves us enough to allow us to leave and even to reject him, but he also loves us enough to welcome us back with a huge party the moment we come home.

Don't believe the fearful and insecure claims that God's gonna get you, punish you, torture you. Some, because of their own failure to trust love, have created a god in their own image—a mean, mad sky bully who hates those they hate, fights on their side against those different from them. Don't buy it. Don't let them scare and manipulate you. We're not sinners in the hands of an angry God, but children in the arms of an adoring dad.

Because my own earthly father was loving, nurturing, and generous, I never had any difficulty experiencing God as abba, but it has been as a dad myself that I have most fully understood God's love. Like a character on a movie screen, I witnessed my dad only externally. However, like a fully developed character in a novel, in becoming a dad, I have experienced abba from within. As a father, I am no longer limited to the outward actions of fatherhood, but the internal ones as well. I've felt the absolutely indescribable joy of holding my children and covering them with kisses. I've heard my own interior monologue of care and concern. I've felt as a father what I could not possibly convey to my children nor could I have understood merely as a child and not a parent.

As a dad, I have learned the truest meaning of love. I love my precious children in a way that I love no other beings in creation. They are far more important to me than me. If God loves me like I love them, then I am truly loved. And God does love me far more than I am capable of loving my children. Both in quality and quantity.

Not all dads are good, and some actually hinder us from experiencing God as abba. Our own dads are the context with which we interpret the metaphor. If we have experienced rejection, abuse, abandonment, or absence from our earthly fathers, it's likely we'll project those negative associations onto our heavenly dad. It's possible to move past them, but it will likely require counseling, recovery work, meditation, and perhaps even surrogate earthly fathers. It's even possible Jesus had to address some of the same issues. The young boy who was known as Mary's little bastard was able to overcome his illegitimacy and fatherlessness through his experience of God as abba—who knows, those feelings may be part of what inspired the intensely intimate relationship.

Throughout his life, in all his teachings, actions, and stories, Jesus insisted that the relationship he had with Abba is available for everyone. God loves us all equally. We are all the children of God. We can have what Jesus had—an intense, intimate, fulfilling, inspiring, purpose-producing relationship with Dad. It's up to us.

One word.

One little word is all we need.

Abba.

Like a scared child in a dark room on a moonless night, all we have to do is say: Daddy? Are you there? He is. Everything's okay. Daddy's home. In fact, Daddy is home, and if we're not, all we have to do is return.

Compassion's Womb

Contrary to popular religion, Jesus said the most central characteristic of God and of Jesus's followers isn't righteousness or holiness, faith or belief, but compassion. Though what Jesus said on the subject is often translated as, Be perfect as God is perfect, what Jesus actually said was, Be compassionate as God is compassionate. In saying so, Jesus, perhaps the first recorded feminist, was calling God our mother.

Mother is the name for God in the hearts of children the world over.

It's possible to summarize Jesus's entire message by saying, God is like a mother full of compassion for her children and we should be the same. It's another way of saying, Love God with all you have and your neighbor as yourself.

The word *compassion* in Hebrew is the plural of a noun that in its singular form means womb. Thus, every time Jesus said God was compassionate, he was actually saying that she was like a womb.

Compassion comes from two Greek words that mean to feel with. *Passion* means to feel and the prefix *com* means with. Compassion occurs when we are deeply moved to the point of actually feeling with a person what she is feeling. This in turn moves us to action on behalf of that person. Jesus was often described as being moved with compassion for the multitudes. He experienced the pain of their sicknesses and the desperation of their hunger, which in turn led him to heal the sick and feed the hungry.

A mother feels compassion for the children of her womb. She actually experiences sensations in her womb—joy when her children are happy, pain when they are sad.

Two mothers, one child. One is the true mother, one has lost her child and is attempting to steal the living child. When the wise King Solomon threatened to cut the baby in half and give each woman part of the child, he discovered who the baby actually belonged to. His threat was a wise test—the test of motherhood, of compassion. The true mother of the living son was moved in her womb with the feeling of compassion for the son of her womb and cried for him to live, even if it had to be with another woman, but the other cried for the child's death.

Compassion, the most motherly of qualities, is a feeling and an action motivated by that feeling. The feeling alone is merely pity, but true compassion, while beginning with this same feeling, cannot stop without moving into action. God is like a mother because her womb-like love causes her to feel deeply all that we, her children, feel. We were all once connected so intimately with her inside her womb (or perhaps, as the Kabala and other sacred writings teach, we still are)—that all of creation is still within the womb of God, growing, developing, waiting to be born.

Our Mom not only nurtures, but shares deep wisdom. She is Sophia, the intuitive wisdom of the feminine. She knows and

feels what we need, what is best for us. She not only has wisdom
to teach us, wisdom to give us—she *is* that wisdom. Listen to this
poem in praise of Sophia:

Does not wisdom call out? Does not understanding raise her voice? On
the heights along the way, where the paths meet, she takes her stand; beside
the gates leading into the city, at the entrances she cries aloud . . . The Lord
brought me forth as the first of his works, before his deeds of old; I was
appointed from eternity, from the beginning, before the world began.

It's obvious that Mary was a central figure in the life of Jesus,
the only one present at the beginning and end of his life. Though
their relationship seemed strained at times, it was her unconditional love, even in the midst of her misunderstandings about her son,
that inspired his concept of God as our heavenly mother. Mary
as a metaphor for Mother God began with Jesus, but continues to
this day among many Christians, particularly Roman Catholics. In a
religion where women can't be priestesses or be involved in church
leadership, there lingers a hint of the feminine face of God. Mary
completes the family of God portrait with her son Jesus and his
abba. This is most obvious in her title, Mother of God, but because Mother God is not in her rightful place, her kindness and
compassion are not central.

They say you can always tell someone who grew up without
a mother. The effects are undeniable. The church is producing
motherless children. The loss is as undeniable as it is catastrophic.
Without bonding with our heavenly mother, we are adrift, less
attached, less whole. We live with insecurities, mistrust, and fear.
Wounded, we are incapable of experiencing compassion for others. Lacking a mother's love, we are empty inside.

Compassion is the heart of true religion. By denying the feminine face of God, by oppressing and subjugating women, male-
dominated religion has lost its soul. How different Jesus's mes-

sage is from that of the church. Jesus's God, the mother hen who desires nothing more than to gather her chicks beneath her wings, has been replaced by a severe, masculine, cosmic judge who uses the threat of punishment to scare people into obedience. Religion has lost compassion. We have lost Jesus's gospel. We have lost God, and, in the process, we have become motherless children, orphans who have lost our identities, our purpose, and the empathy for one another a mother's love enables us to experience.

Contamination

How did we lose the way? How was the message of Jesus replaced? The only way it could be.

When I was growing up, my family owned a sod farm. It didn't look like much. In fact, it so resembled an empty field that when I brought one of my friends home from college he asked, Where are the sods? I don't see anything but grass.

Growing grass (the legal kind anyway) makes for an interesting crop. Perhaps what makes sod so remarkable is its resiliency. Unlike other crops, it's extremely difficult to destroy. If burned, the grass will grow back—often more green and lush than before. If part of the sod is removed, the remaining parts will spread across the missing section, growing back together, replacing what was excised. Even if the grass dies, turning yellowish and hay-like from drought or brown and brittle from frost, it will come to life again with the next rainfall or the return of warm weather.

About the only thing that threatens a sod crop is contamination. Only seeds from other types of grass or weeds can alter it.

What Rome's reign of torture and murder couldn't quench, its adopting the way and adding to and taking away from it did. Rome only won its war against the Jesus movement once it made Christianity the official religion of the empire, and what Jesus's first followers couldn't understand and stop, they could change and contaminate.

Forcing Jesus into a religion has so altered and diluted him that the Christ of Christianity bears little resemblance to Jesus of Nazareth. Religion—particularly the more organized and systematic forms—is so clearly a human invention. God is love and life and Jesus was ablaze with them both. He is a poem, a transformative sacred story, a force. Like life, the true Jesus can't be contained inside a religion. The way flows like a river. Religion is a dam attempting to control it. It prunes and shapes and injuriously cuts the tree of life. It makes of the book of life a blunt how-to text or simplistic owner's manual.

From the very beginning, Jesus's message and meaning was not only missed and misunderstood, but it was framed and changed, commented on, added to and subtracted from, translated and interpreted. In the process, which continues millennia later, Jesus's message has been lost, obscured, hidden, and in some cases hijacked.

Many scholars are convinced that parts of what's in the Gospels, all of which were written several decades after Jesus died, are contaminated. They find in them examples of writers, who were struggling with the Pharisees and others, putting words in the mouth of Jesus that he never spoke, reflecting their own theology, agendas, and even animosity with other Jewish sects. The search for the authentic Jesus and his teachings has led to the specialty of Jesus scholarship and organizations like the Jesus Seminar.

Scholars point to anti-Semitism, prophecy written as history, as well as sayings that contradict the heart and essence of Jesus's message as evidence of contamination—and this recognition is not a recent phenomenon. So convinced was Thomas Jefferson that the true Jesus had been contaminated by his first biographers and evangelists, that he created his own Bible by cutting out only the passages he believed to be authentic and pasting them into a new book.

Speaking of the Gospels, Jefferson says: In the New Testament there is internal evidence that parts of it have proceeded from an extraordinary man; and that other parts are of the fabric of very inferior minds. It is as easy to separate those parts as to pick out diamonds from dunghills. We must reduce our volume to the simple evangelists, select, even from them, the very words only of Jesus, paring off the amphibologisms into which they have been led by forgetting often, or not understanding, what had fallen from him, by giving their own misconceptions as his dicta, and expressing unintelligibly for others what they had not understood themselves. There will be found remaining the most sublime and benevolent code of morals which has ever been offered to man.

Paul, and those writing under his name, framed Christianity from the very beginning. His letters were circulated decades prior to the Gospels. Thus, people were told who Jesus was and what he meant before hearing his own words, witnessing his own actions. This has led many to conclude that Christianity is far more the religion of Paul than of Jesus.

Of course, we all contaminate the teachings of Jesus (despite my best efforts, I'm doing it right now). The key is to alter Jesus and his message as little as possible, to be aware we're doing it, hear the spirit and not merely the letter of what is being said, and to avoid changing things so completely that it changes the meaning.

When Jesus's words and life are filtered through our prejudices, paradigms, and biases, they are changed. This happened with his first followers, his first biographers, evangelists, and interpreters, and it continues until this very day. However, this is not what causes Jesus's gospel to be lost or hidden nearly so much as those who actually say things Jesus never said; refuse to take actions he said should be taken; live in ways contrary to his teachings; add to and subtract from his message; actually create an entirely new religion and name it after him. This goes beyond common human failure to betrayal and treason, and it's this more than anything else that causes us to lose the gospel of Jesus.

There are many ways to understand the extraordinary life of Jesus of Nazareth, but the one that has dominated from the beginning is viewing him through ancient Israel's sacrificial system. Paul and those writing under his name said that Jesus was both high priest and sacrificial lamb, that his entire life was about being sacrificed by God for the sins of humanity. The result of this guilt and propitiation framing of the life of Jesus is a Christian religion that primarily seeks to persuade people to accept the sacrifice made on their behalf and tell others so they can also. This contamination and oversimplification of Jesus's message causes his gospel to be lost, replacing it with the gospel of Paul and the church. Rather than a lifestyle, Christianity has become a belief system whereby someone is saved by acknowledging their sinfulness and accepting Jesus's sacrificial payment for that sin. Instead of living the gospel of Jesus (caring for the poor and oppressed, seeking justice for everyone, truly loving our enemies, and sharing our possessions) we spread the gospel about Jesus, telling people what he did on our behalf, not viewing his life as an example of how we should live.

Nothing contaminates more than the corrupting influence of power. Christianity lost its way a long time ago when it was se-

duced by power. Instead of seeking to serve like Jesus, the powerful Christian church seeks to be served, expecting people to bow
before it as much as the God it represents (after all, it sees itself
as the embodiment of that God on earth). Inquisitions, crusades,
abuse—all occur as Christians gain power, forget the true mission
to serve, forget that we are responsible for the poor and oppressed, actually becoming the oppressors, transforming the cross
into a sword, the humble servant-storyteller into a conquering
general on a white horse setting up his throne in the white house.

As the ones who contaminate the teachings of Jesus, choke
out the seed sown to change the world by our weeds of selfishness, greed, ambition, and thirst for power, we are the ones who
can stop it. We can recover Jesus's message, uncover his truth and
wisdom, and begin to live the way he did.

How can we find the true, uncontaminated teachings of Jesus? How do we prevent the words of others—in and out of the
Bible—from obscuring his words? We could create our own Bible
as Thomas Jefferson famously did, excising everything but what he
believed to be Jesus's words. We could go with what scholars, like
those of the Jesus Seminar, say are the authentic words of Jesus.
We could just read the words in red for a while. However we do
it, we must hear and see. We must remove the contamination, the
corruption, reject anything that doesn't line up with the character
and spirit of Jesus—even when it's in the Bible or declared from a
pulpit.

The Non-Religious Rabbi and Religion of the Heart

Jesus stood against and even attacked virtually every aspect of outward religion—opposing public prayer and visible fasting, ritual purification, Sabbath observations, ritual sacrifice, the temple sacrificial system, the temple itself, the priesthood, religious leaders, and all the major sects of his day, including the Pharisees, Sadducees, and Scribes.

When you pray, he said, don't be like the religious, who prefer to pray in religious settings and public places so others can see them. Go into a secret place and close the doors and windows so you can truly commune with God.

Over and over Jesus insisted that the thing that keeps people from God the most is religion. The Sabbath was made for man, not man for the Sabbath. You're serving religion instead of living in love. Why do you make rules and observances? Why do you focus on what can be seen? Who are you doing these things for?

Do you think God wants external sacrifices? Do you think God has an ego and wants to be worshiped? These things you do for yourself and others. God wants your heart. God wants you to live in love, to stand with the oppressed not the powerful and self-righteous.

He railed against outward displays of devotion, the materialistic, external religion of the self-righteous, calling instead for religion of the heart. For him, religion wasn't about rites and rituals and things that can be seen by others, but about being—about who we are and how we are in the world. It's an inward experience that emanates outward in love and service—not for religious institutions and leaders, but for the least and lowest, the poor, the helpless, the condemned, the outcast, the diseased, the incarcerated, the widow, the orphan.

The outward is not just the most obvious, but the most shallow, the most meaningless. The purely physical fails to perceive the spiritual. It leaves no room for the transcendent.

The Kingdom of God is within you. It's not going to come about by observation. It's not something you can see. It's inside you—and has been all along. Jesus says that the way to God is not outside of us. It's not in synagogues, mosques, and churches, but in the depths of our souls. Religion of the heart is meditative, contemplative. It plumbs the depths of the heart instead of ascending the heights of liturgy. Look within, Jesus says. Go in, go down, go deep. God is there.

Religion of the heart is the antithesis of most of the religion practiced—both in Jesus's day and in our own. Unless your righteousness exceeds that of the Scribes and Pharisees, Jesus said, you will not enter the Kingdom of God.

The Scribes and the Pharisees, like the Puritans and Fundamentalists of our day, were the most outwardly righteous people based on literally keeping their own rules. They were above reproach in matters of laws and regulations. Their devotion was obvious, even extreme. But this kind of religion is so concerned with the outward that it forgets what's most important. Jesus compared this type of religion to whitewashed graves—clean and attractive on the outside, while inside there's rotting flesh and decaying bone.

Jesus said the pure in heart will see God. The outwardly pure will be seen by others and thought to be righteous, religious, but the inwardly clean will see God. To the pure, all things are pure, and God is everywhere, in all things. God's subtlety is best viewed through the eyes of purity, his hiddenness through the eyes of the heart.

As in our day, the religious people of Jesus's time were overly concerned with what people did with their bodies—especially what they put in them—but Jesus taught it's not what goes into us that defiles us, but what comes out—what was in our hearts to begin with.

Outward religion is meant to influence and control our actions, but it can't change our hearts. Through discipline, repression, peer pressure, practice, repetition, we can act in ways contrary to our natures for a limited time, but these things can't change our hearts. Eventually, what's in (greed, hate, racism, judgmentalism, murder) will come out.

Instead of connecting people with God, outward religion actually has the opposite effect. Rules can't create a relationship. Rites and rituals are poor substitutes for intimacy. The priest and the Levite of the parable of the Good Samaritan let their religion prevent them from acting humanely.

Religion of the heart is simple, if not easy: Love God with your whole heart and love people—all people—as much as you love yourself. This is Jesus's message. This is his life. This is his religion.

So how does someone like Jesus become the figurehead of an outward-oriented religion?

It can only happen when people replace his way with their own.

Jesus says everything—absolutely everything—comes down to loving God with all you have, loving yourself, and loving your neighbor as yourself. And we said that's not enough. We want a religion. We want codes and creeds. We want things we have to believe and do, things that we can mark off a list, things that will keep us separate from others.

In the same way that ancient Israel looked around at all the other nations and said, We want a king, we want to be like them, the followers of Jesus have said we want a religion. We want reward and punishment—not unconditional love, not grace. We want rites and rituals, not secret prayer. We want to have a group, to define ourselves and others, to exclude the others, to continue to be tribal—not oneness, not true unconditional love. Give us religion.

Jesus says we can be free. We say we don't want to be free. But you are. Thank you, but we prefer our little boxes. We'd rather have our comfortable old paradigms.

Jesus says God's gifts are free. We say we want to work for them. But they're free, like God's love. You can't earn love. You can't deserve grace. So here we are working hard in the wrong ways for something we already have, something that's been ours all along, something we refuse to receive.

Jesus offers a way of love, a way to God that is inner, not outer, that is about relating, not religion, and we immediately set about to make a religion out of it, to alter Jesus's message and the meaning of his life so as to fit it into a systematic theology, a world religion that looks like and acts like and is too like all other religions.

How do you form a religion around a figure who attacked religion? Ironically, in the case of Jesus, his followers adopted the very religious practices he stood against, forcing an anti-religious revolutionary to become the namesake for the very things he opposed. Paul framed it in the context of ancient Judaism, through the patriarchs and prophets all the way to the sacrificial system that Jesus attacked, and a religion was born.

Think about it. Jesus taught there was no need for sacrifices, that the ancient, superstitious notions of appeasing the gods with blood sacrifices were ridiculous—wrong on every level. God doesn't want a virgin or a lamb or a bull, doesn't need the offer of these things to accept us. (Do you demand a sacrifice before you accept your children? Your friends and family? Is God less loving than you?)

We are accepted. We are loved. God is love. She loves us unconditionally. She doesn't demand or even want sacrifices. She wants us, wants a relationship with us. And what did we do? We formed a religion in which the man who taught that God doesn't want sacrifices is seen as a sacrifice—the sacrifice for all time—and billions of people have related to him in only that mode ever since. This makes Jesus the most tragically ironic figure in all of history.

Jesus offered new wine and we forced it into old wineskins. Jesus offered a way—the way to God, to life, to love—and we chose our old paradigms and prison cells instead.

We choose guilt and expiation over love and relationship.

We choose working and earning over receiving the free gift of grace.

We choose self-imposed prison sentences over true freedom.

We choose things that divide rather than unite.

We choose outward religion over inner.

Jesus calls us to experience religion of the heart, to a kingdom that is not of this world and so doesn't operate in the ways of this world, can't be thought of in the same ways the things of this world can be.

Your religious practices you're doing for yourself and others, not God.

Give up your religion and find God.

Stop letting your religion keep you from God.

True religion is not outward, not some rite or ritual, not an observation or attendance, not doctrine or dogma, not simple beliefs or creeds. The Kingdom of God is inside you. God loves you and wants you to experience true, unconditional love and then live inside it, sharing it with others. Not very religious, I realize— just true. You are accepted. You are loved. How will you respond to this free gift? By attempting to pay for it? With what? Belief? Observation? Attendance? Charity? Superiority? Exclusion? What will you use to buy what is not for sale and you already have?

Lost and Found

Ironically, Jesus's message of radical love and freedom are most often found and most often lost in the same place—the Bible.

Whether viewed from a literary or religious perspective, the sheer power of the Bible is undeniable. It is perhaps the most influential book in human history. But of all the accolades that can be accorded it, it's as the vessel through which Jesus is revealed that it is most praiseworthy, most beneficial to humanity. Conversely, it is in the ways that it fails to reveal Jesus, the ways in which it actually conceals Jesus, his spirit, his message, that the Bible does the most damage, becomes the most dangerous.

Violations of the Bible—from simple-minded literalism to self-serving manipulation—are so numerous and occur with such frequency that they are the rule, not the exception. No other book has been more misused and abused—partly because of what it contains, but largely because of what's in the hearts and minds of those who use it. How we read the Bible and which parts of it we gravitate toward reveal far more about us than they do the Bible.

The Bible is a literary patchwork quilt—what various people at different times have said about God, and it's more about the people who created it than it is about the God they're writing about. Through their writings, we view biblical authors' hopes and fears, their beliefs and doubts about God, and through them, a sketchy picture of God emerges. Parts of the Bible seem to rise to the level of the sublime, God in the form of words, while other parts fall flat, thudding to the earth in their bluntness and misperception.

The Bible is not a single book, but a library of books written by hundreds of people in several cultures and languages over thousands of years. The Bible is a gathering of writings that form a conceptual composite of God.

Because the Bible is bound like any other single book, and because numerous common threads are woven throughout its rich tapestry, many people make the mistake of viewing, reading, and interpreting the Bible as a single volume. This would be similar to walking into a public library and reading all the books the same way. You don't read a dictionary the way you do a novel or a volume of poetry, and you don't read them for the same reasons. Each has a purpose. Each has its own conventions. Each must be approached in a different way. So it is with the Bible.

Many of the stories of the Bible were oral and were told around campfires for hundreds of years before they were ever written down. Some of the books of the Bible were originally letters written from a prison cell addressing a particular congregation or person dealing with particular issues and concerns. Some of the books were written in narrative and prose, others in poetry and song. Some of the Bible was written in Hebrew, some of it in Greek, but none of it was written in English.

The Bible is not a textbook, not a how-to, self-help guide, not a treatise on spirituality or an answer book to life's toughest questions, nor is it a manual of morality. It's a literary masterpiece whose subtle, often sublime truths must be understood in the context of the literary devices its authors chose to employ.

To view the Bible as purely divine is to elevate it to an object worthy of worship and place demands on it that it simply wasn't meant to bear. When we begin to focus on the Bible rather than what it reveals, it is like fixing our sight on a cloudy windowpane rather than the beautiful day that can be seen through it.

In certain subtle ways, the Bible reveals God, but much of what is recorded is the projection onto God—the hopes and fears, preferences and prejudices—of the writers.

The Bible reveals God to us indirectly and metaphorically. Through it, we hear the thoughts of those who've gone before us, and in their finest moments, the voice of God actually echoes within theirs.

A purely literal approach to the Bible not only misses all the truly remarkable subtle and sublime truths that make the texts sacred, but it's also extremely dangerous.

Literalism is the single most dangerous way to misread, misinterpret, and misapply the Bible. True, there are many other ways to misread, misinterpret, and misapply the Bible, but none of them are as harmful and destructive as literalism.

When read literally, the Bible depicts God as self-contradictory—at times a wrathful tyrant, at times a patient parent, and everything in between. So anthropomorphized God has been by his biographers that he embodies all human characteristics and contradictions simultaneously.

Literalism divorces the Bible from its cultural context, taking isolated words and literally interpreting their surface meaning.

This violent rape of the sacred writ has led to the justification of crusades, inquisitions, the Holocaust, murder, racism, segregation, tribalism, hate, violence, and many other inhumane horrors.

As a composite of ancient theological writings, the Bible attempts to reveal God to us, and it does this most clearly and powerfully in those places where the unaltered, authentic Jesus is seen and heard. It is through him, his life and teachings, that we should read and interpret the rest of the Bible—not the other way around, which is most often the case. Jesus is the lens through which it must be read. In Jesus, the distortions and inaccuracies and out of focus sketches of God in the Bible come into sharp relief, the babble becomes clear communication. God is seen. God is heard.

You have heard of old that you should love your neighbor and hate your enemy, but I say that you should love your enemies. Clearly, Jesus says over and over again in his words and actions that the old ways were wrong—that the old concepts of God were inaccurate and dangerous. Early perceptions of God and what she wanted for humanity were just off. The people Jesus addressed actually believed God wanted them to stone disobedient children, to put to death adulterers, farmers who grew the wrong types of crops in the same field, people who wore clothing made from two different types of cloth, and so on.

A god who hates and destroys, a tribal deity or nationalistic god (which is actually a composite of many different gods from Yahweh, to El, to Elohim, to Shaddai), is not compatible with Jesus's Abba. But rather than choosing between these two distinct views of God found in the Bible, many people, including devout Christians, just incorporate Abba in with all the others to form a manic-depressive, schizophrenic, twisted sadist who is all too human in his rants and temper tantrums, his hatred and lack of forgiveness, his destruction and punishment, and repenting and relenting.

The consequence of misreading and misinterpreting Jesus in the light of the Bible instead of the other way around is loss. What is lost is our best glimpse of God. We lose Jesus, we lose God, we lose love and freedom. We lose everything—including our very souls.

Love and Freedom

It's early and quiet, a soft glow illuminates the moist morning, but the sun has yet to rise above the rim of the earth.

Jesus is alone.

As usual, he has risen early and sought out a solitary place. Quiet communion devoid of distraction is worth the sacrifice of sleep.

The previous day, word spread through the town of Capernaum that he was at Simon's home, and by sunset the sick, diseased, and dying had been brought to him. Laying his hands on each one, he freed them from their diseases.

Weary, spent, he is seeking the restorative connection of meditation, silence, and prayer—healing of his own.

As soon as the townspeople awaken and realize he is missing, they begin to search for him. When they finally find him, they beg and plead and try to convince him to stay:

You can't leave us now. We need you. Please stay. Please. We'll do anything to get you to stay. What do you want? We'll get it for you.

I must proclaim the good news of the Kingdom of God to the other towns also, Jesus replied, for this is why I was sent.

This happened nearly everywhere Jesus went. Everyone in his life pressured him to be what they wanted him to be, to do what they wanted him to do—all of them attempting to exert control over him. The political and religious leaders continually attempted to force him to conform; his followers and friends constantly tried to persuade him to get off his path; and his family, who had tried to mold and manipulate him his whole life, ultimately tried to physically restrain and arrest him.

Freedom is exemption from external control, interference, and regulation, the power to determine action without restraint. Jesus lived free from the control and restraint of others. He lived free from conformity to cultural and religious traditions—continually communicating and demonstrating how those things too quickly become taskmasters that enslave rather than liberate, how rules and regulations, whether about Sabbath or sacrifice, are snares that entrap us, having an effect opposite of their original intent.

Religion is not something commonly associated with freedom. In fact, the reverse is usually the case. But Jesus's message is one of freedom—true and absolute freedom, compassion our sole guide. His is a religion with one rule—treat others as you'd like to be treated.

He not only lived in absolute freedom, but taught that true religion is freeing.

For him, true freedom is the organic outgrowth of a life of love.

Love and freedom are inseparable. You can't have one without the other.

The very word *freedom* comes from a root that means to love. We must be free in order to love.

Freedom is the fuel of love's flame. The more freedom, the more love. And few things extinguish love as fast as freedom's absence.

Jesus's love-centered life was one of absolute freedom—freedom from culture, religion, and the control of others, including family and friends and those in political and religious power, but mostly freedom from fear.

Few things alter, distort, or imprison us like fear. Freedom from fear is foundational to all freedom. Love makes us free from fear, is the only thing that can make us truly free.

Jesus lived a life free from fear because he was so secure in love, in God, in his identity, in his mission.

Being secure in love opens us, enables us to become our best, most original selves—free to think, to explore, to experiment, to risk, to truly be authentic. Fear causes us to close, to shrink, to wither, but love leads us to be open, to blossom, to thrive.

Like Jesus, we can only be truly and completely ourselves— when we're free. When we're free from threat, free from fear, free from condemnation, free from disapproval, free from the cultural and parental programming inside our heads, can we be who we were intended to be.

Of all our fears, the greatest and most foundational is the fear of death.

By conquering his fear of death through absolute trust in love, Jesus found true freedom. The path he offers is the way of freedom, the way of finding our own way, free from fear, secure in love, open in the way only truly free people can be.

Perfect love casts out all fear.

Love lets go. Fear clings to—often to the point of suffocation. In the same way love and freedom are inseparable, love and fear are incompatible.

Love creates. Lack of freedom destroys. Creativity requires freedom. Art is an act of love created in the womb of freedom. Jesus not only taught freedom, he lived it. He did this because of his image of God.

God, who is love, gives us the greatest gift of all—freedom to love, freedom to reject love.

God's radical commitment to our freedom is the greatest evidence that God is love. God never forces us to take action, never makes us do anything—only continually creates a universe filled with choices. You and I can love God or we can hate God, we can trust God or doubt God—including God's very existence.

What are the two trees in the center of the story of the Garden of Eden—one of life, the other of the knowledge of good and evil—if not symbols of freedom, of choice. The choices represented by the trees aren't hidden away. God created the choices and placed them prominently in the garden.

Out of love, God created a world where there is the possibility of love, but only the possibility, only the freedom to create the world we want, to be the people we want to be—to be the lovers we want to be. But we can also be insecure possessors or indifferent, defensive cynics. We're granted the freedom to be. What we become is up to us.

Love is risky. Manipulation, control, force, guilt—all seem to be more effective, and may even produce the desired behavior, but they won't produce love. They can't. Only love and the freedom to return that love can truly produce love.

Jesus spent his life as a freedom fighter—someone who lived in freedom and continually helped others do the same.

Jesus freed the woman caught in adultery from condemnation—as he did all the hookers and pimps and drunks and unclean
and impure he hung out with. He freed his students from ignorance and fear and slavish servitude to tradition. He also freed
them from easy moralizing and a materialistic religion: You have
heard it was said of old not to kill, but I say to you don't even hate.
It's not what can be seen, not the outward, but the inward, the hidden, the heart.

He freed his followers from rules and regulations and religious
duty—telling them to pray and do charity in private, to break silly
Sabbath ordinances that prevented them from doing good and
acting compassionately and doing justice. Man wasn't made for the
Sabbath, but Sabbath for man. He freed them from external religion, criticizing the purity system that labeled and divided everything into clean and unclean, pure and impure, telling them
God does not desire sacrifice or observance, but our hearts—true
worship is in the complete freedom of spirit and truth, not tradition, formality, rites, rituals, rules and regulations. Outward purity
is nothing. Inward purity is everything. Be free to love—love God
with all your heart, love others as you love yourself. Be free from
religion that actually prevents you from doing these things by replacing love with checklists of outward morality and actions taken
for appearance.

How tragic it is when, in our attempt to follow Jesus, we fail
to be free, when we revert back to the prison of spiritless religion,
allowing others who do not practice Jesus's religion of the heart to
enslave us in his name.

Freedom can be scary when we're accustomed to fear. We
reject it for the comfort of the cell, the safety of the crowd, the
reassurance of rituals and rules. But these things are not life, are
not love, are not free, are not of Jesus or his message.

Take the risk. Be love. Be free. Don't let fear win. Don't give in to cultural conventions, external religions, or the seeming safety of the herd. Find your way again along the way—the way of love and freedom. It's the only way to be our most unique, authentic, idiosyncratic, best selves.

The Greatest Stories Ever Told

Of all that has been lost or hidden, obscured or ignored, it's the stories Jesus told that are most absent from the hollow modern gospel.

The parables of Jesus are insightful, witty, and as true as anything ever uttered from a human mouth, but they are also challenging, explosive, and subversive—calling into question every assumption, all we believe and hold dear, all our conventional wisdom, our very foundations. No wonder these life-altering, potentially world-changing stories of Jesus have been replaced with sentimental stories about him.

Story is the language of God. It's the language of life, of experience. It is present in all the languages of the world. It's a human language, told in human terms, made meaningful through symbol, myth, and metaphor.

Stories speak a transcendent language. They capture us emotionally as well as intellectually, drawing us into their world from the very first word. Unlike non-narrative sentences, we can actually enter inside stories. When Jesus says, A man had two sons, right away we know we can become either the father or the older or the younger son. Or maybe even all three. Facts and figures are opaque, but stories are transparent. We embark on stories, actually entering them, becoming a character, taking the journey. The truth we receive from them, we receive from within, experiencing them like dreams, through our imaginations, staying submerged until The End.

Stories speak to the most powerful part of us—our imaginations. They tap into the hidden potential of our ability to fantasize and imagine. No other form of communication can so fully engage us, nothing else speaks so directly to our cores.

Stories speak of a truth beyond facts and events. All stories are true, and some of them actually happened. This is important to remember when we're listening to the language of God. Truth and fact are not the same thing. A story is not true because it actually happened, it is true because it tells a truth, it resonates inside us as authentic and accurate. If we disqualify stories for not being factually true, then all stories are disqualified, and we miss the whole point of stories to begin with, which is not to inform, but to transform.

What science, history, and law cannot do, story can. The mystical and mythical properties of story leave room for truth, for God. Good stories can be so insightful, so absolutely true, so nuanced, so subtle, so sublime, that the whispered voice of God echoes within them.

If story is the language of God, no one in human history has ever spoken it more fluently than Jesus. As much as anything else, Jesus was a teller of scandalous stories—tales that shocked, offended, jarred his listeners, even as they rocked the foundation of their world.

In its rejection of the gospel of Jesus in favor of the gospel about Jesus, Christianity has ignored, or worse, domesticated and castrated the parables, those embers that threaten to ignite a fire it can't control or profit from, a blaze that would engulf the world.

Uncovering the lost gospel of Jesus means not just listening, but hearing and understanding his subversive stories, entering the dream, allowing it to have its way with us.

Forget What You've Heard

Forget what you've heard. Let me tell you what God is really like. God is like a man with two sons. One day the younger of the two came to his dad and asked for his part of their inheritance. Implicit in the son's request is the wish for his father's death. In essence the son says, Dad, I'm tired of waiting around here for you to die. How about giving me my money now, so I can get on with my life?

It's a startling thing for a son to say, but what is far more shocking is that his dad actually divides up what he has (what he lives on and how he makes a living) and gives the younger son his portion.

Not long after the younger son got what he thought was his freedom ('cause nothin' says do what the hell you want like a stash of cash), he packed up what he had and hit the road—not just down the block or across town, but to another country, getting as far away from his dad as he could. The message was clear, the rejection total, the pain complete.

In this foreign land, away from his dad and his dad's watchful eyes, he threw the largest, longest-running party in history until that time. He had all the friends, booze, drugs, and women he could ever want—until his money ran out.

Out of money, out of friends, and out of luck, what's a poor little rich boy to do? Out of desperation, he tries to get a job. His dad's a farmer. His stupid-ass brother helps him. How hard could it be? He hires on as a pig feeder. It was as low as he could go—or so he thought. Pigs stank, the work was dirty, what he had to feed them would trigger anybody's gag reflexes, and enough of his dad's religion had rubbed off for him to feel that the pigs were cursed, unclean, forbidden. But all this wasn't the worst of it. The absolute worst, the thudding sound of him hitting his absolute bottom, was when he was so hungry that the shit he was feeding the pigs began to look tasty to him.

What the hell am I doing? My dad's servants eat better than this. I'll go home and tell the old man that I was wrong. Tell him I don't deserve to be his son, but I could be one of his slaves.

Not out of a change of heart or true repentance, but because of circumstances, because of desperation, because of a lack of options, he returns home. His older brother's right, he'll never change. He's a user, a spoiled loser, irresponsible, good for nothin'.

Out of money, a failure, he's going home. No surprises there. But as we've seen earlier in our story, we can count on the father for a surprise. He's the only one who acts in unexpected ways— and here's a shocker.

When his dad sees his young son walking down the long road to their house, he jumps up and runs toward him—something the son's never seen his dad do. As he reaches him, he doesn't hit him, there's no anger on his face. He doesn't even let his son finish the

apology he's rehearsed before calling for new clothes to replace
the filthy rags he's wearing, a new family ring to replace the one he
hawked, and ordering a huge party to be thrown in honor of his
son's return.

To recap: Wish your father dead, waste everything he worked
hard to give you on pot and prostitutes, reject him, hurt him, put
him through hell, and what do you get? Not so much as an I told
you so, just overwhelming love. A love so complete, so perfect,
so unconditional that it could only be lavished on someone who
really, *really* doesn't deserve it. Forget what you've been told about
God. This is who he is. No anger. No wrath. No preaching. No
human pettiness or need for retaliation. God is grace. God is
mercy. God is unconditional love.

When the older brother returns from a very hard day in the
fields and hears all the music and laughter coming from inside
the house, he asks one of the servants what the hell is going on.
Has the old man finally lost his mind? Upon hearing that the self-
centered little bastard who's wasted their money and embarrassed
their family has come home and his dad is so happy he's throw-
ing him a party, he's so pissed he won't even go inside the house.
Hearing this, his dad leaves his party and goes out in search of his
older son. He doesn't send an order for him to get his ass inside
the house now, doesn't send someone else after him, but goes himself.

How could you do this? the older son asks his dad. Can't you
see what a slap in the face this is to me, how disrespectful? Here
I have worked for you like a slave all these years and you've never
even thrown a small party for me and my friends, and this little
spoiled brat comes home after squandering everything and you
throw him the frickin' party of the century.

With kindness and patience every bit as gracious as with the
younger son, the father explains to the older, self-righteous son

how everything he has belongs to both sons and he could have had a party any time he wanted. I hope you can understand, the father explains. I have to celebrate. My son was lost and now is found, was dead and now is alive again. I'd do the same if it were you.

Most scholars believe that the first hearers of Jesus's story would have related far more to the older brother than the younger. They believed themselves to be righteous, people who earned God's love by their work. And though they had never left, never rebelled, they were just as lost as the younger brother—but in worse shape because they didn't know it and because their false sense of earned self-righteousness prevented them from feeling compassion for their lost little brother. Even still, the father expresses just as much unconditional love, just as much mercy, just as much compassion for them.

Forget what you've heard. God is not what you've been taught. God is love—perfect, complete, no-strings-attached, unconditional love. Whether we are irresponsible or overly responsible, party too much or not at all, waste all we have or hoard it, whether we ever truly feel remorse and repent or never do, God loves us. If we've rejected him and live as far away from him as we can, we're still his children and he still loves us. If we say we're near him, never stray far from his side, yet don't really even know him, don't understand or act like him, we're still his children, still loved beyond all reason.

Forget what you've heard. Embrace the outrageous and absurd. You are loved perfectly and completely. No matter what. You can't do anything to lose this love any more than you did anything to earn it. It's not based on you or your actions or your prayers or your obedience. It's just who your father is. Know him or not, believe it or not. God is love. You are loved—even if you can't forget what you've heard.

Half Dead in a Ditch

If loving God and loving our neighbors are the two most important things we can ever do, are, in fact, the greatest of all commandments, and if loving our neighbors is the only way we have of demonstrating that we really love God, then the whole of what Jesus taught was to love our neighbors, and it's not at all unreasonable to ask, Exactly who the hell are our neighbors?—which is exactly what an expert in the law of Moses did.

You say I am responsible for certain people, that I should care for and love them as much as I do myself, so who are these people?

In Jesus's day, as in ours, social, political, and religious divisions kept people apart. People were separated into groups and categories. In fact, as divided as we are today along lines of race and class and religion, Jesus's day was far worse. In his day, everyone and everything was categorized as clean or unclean, pure or impure, righteous or wicked, blessed or cursed. It's no wonder the lawyer wanted clarification on exactly who his neighbor was.

To answer the man, Jesus did what he most often did. He told a story.

A certain man was traveling from Jerusalem to Jericho, a seventeen-mile stretch of barren desert and rocky hill country known as the Way of Blood because of how many thugs and gangs hid along it picking off travelers, robbing, raping, and killing them. The temple, and therefore the center of Jewish life and religion, was in Jerusalem, while Jericho was a thriving, wealthy city with a lot of trade. The Way of Blood was well traveled, often by people with money.

The man of our story traveling this dangerous road was attacked by a gang, robbed, stripped, beaten nearly to death, left in the ditch to die. Remember those categories I mentioned earlier? A dead body was considered extremely unclean, able to defile anyone who came in contact with it.

But things are going to be okay. By chance, a certain priest was going the same way. Thank God. How fortunate for our poor half-dead man that a man of God just happened to be traveling his way. We can all breathe a sigh of relief because help has arrived—or has it?

Seeing the man, the priest pretends he doesn't, crosses to the other side of the road, passes by, and keeps on trucking. Shocking! A priest won't stop to help a fellow Jew. Why? Obviously, he doesn't want to be defiled. He's a holy man. Purity and cleanliness are what matter most in his religion. Besides, he's probably on his way to the temple, to serve God. He doesn't have time to mess with this man, who's probably dead anyway.

Everybody knows professional clergy are corrupt, right? So it's fortunate for our man half dead in the ditch that a lay leader of his religion, a Levite, happens along. Here's someone who serves God not because he's paid, not because he gets to wield power over the people, but because he loves God. Surely he will help. But he, too,

crosses to the other side and passes by, anxious not to defile himself, just wanting to serve God. Besides, what if the robbers are
still around? It's the man's fault anyway. If he hadn't been where he
was or doing what he was doing or wearing what he was wearing,
this wouldn't have happened. Hate to say it, but it's his own damn
fault. Obviously, he's not right with God or God wouldn't have al-
lowed it.

So for primarily religious reasons, the priest and the lay leader
pass by without offering assistance. They're on their way to the
temple or on their way back from it. They've got more God stuff
to do. They don't want to become unclean, impure. If they violate
God's laws of cleanliness and purity they could lose God's favor
and protection and wind up like the man half dead in the ditch.

Remember also the man is naked, stripped of everything that
could identify him. There's no way for the priest or the Levite to
know whether the man is one of them, part of their tribe, group,
religious, cultural, socio-economic, pure, closed circle. My God, he
could be anybody! Can't take a chance.

After these two devout men have gone, a certain Samaritan
happens upon the scene, and you know what that means? The
half-dead man in the ditch can bend a little bit more and kiss his
ass goodbye. No way in hell a dirty, half-breed, infidel Samaritan
bastard's gonna do anything but spit in his direction. Jews hate
Samaritans and Samaritans aren't too fond of Jews. They're not of
the same race, don't practice the same religion, don't live the same
way. Dude, when it rains it frickin' pours. Talk about a streak of
bad luck. Man's already been robbed and beaten and left for dead,
but his last hope of help is his worst enemy.

Jesus's original audience likely expected the list of travelers to
be a priest, a Levite, and then an Israelite. Let a regular Joseph save
the day, a common man, a man of the people. But a Samaritan?
What the hell?

Instead of passing on by or spitting on him or seeing if there was anything left to steal, the Samaritan rushes over to the man, bandages his wounds, puts him on his own beast and takes him to the closest hotel, and pays for his full recovery.

Shock! Awe! Scandal!

This isn't a sweet little story about being a good neighbor, but a scathing indictment of a certain type of religion, of dividing people into categories of pure and impure, clean and unclean, of nearly everything those who claim to follow Jesus have become.

Religion, Jesus shows, can actually be the thing that keeps us from being righteous like God. We can get so wrapped up in following the rules that we lose our own souls. Compassion is the primary characteristic of a righteous person, not obedience to orthodoxy or staying clean, however that might be defined.

Words are cheap. Actions demonstrate who we really are. To Jesus's original audience, the Samaritans were lost, deceived, didn't worship and serve the true God (which is to say didn't do it like they did it). They didn't believe the right things, didn't have sound doctrine. Put a Christian in the ditch and the hero of Jesus's story would be a Muslim or a Jew. Put a redneck, homophobic racist in the ditch and the hero of Jesus's story would be an African-American drag queen from Manhattan.

Who is my neighbor? What is the gospel of Jesus? Love is all. Belief, doctrine, clean, unclean, pure, impure, race, class, rich, poor are nothing compared to compassion. A religion that teaches doctrines of purity, that promotes the us-versus-them mentality of nationalism and puts God on our side against everyone else is not compatible with the teachings of Jesus.

The gospel of Jesus is the lifestyle of compassion. It's not letting religion, even that which calls itself by his name, or race, or class, get in the way of compassion. If you were half dead in a ditch somewhere, would you want *you* happening upon the scene?

Are you willing to break your most precious principles, the doctrines to which you're most dedicated, in order to help someone in need? Principles are what people have instead of love and life. Purity systems are what people have instead of pure hearts.

Put your worst enemy in the ditch, the person who has hurt you the most, the person who has wronged you the most, the person you most hate. What would you do? Pass by or stop and help? The person isn't just your sworn enemy. He or she is Jesus, is you.

Speaking Fiction to Power

Like all poor people, Jesus's poverty had a profound effect on him. He was a peasant. The meaning of his life and message cannot be understood without understanding the impact being impoverished had on him. Jesus's family and friends, his neighbors, everyone in his community were poor—and not just poor, but oppressed. Galilean peasantry of Jesus's day were farmers who were systematically exploited by the domination system in place at the time. They worked the land, but didn't profit from it. Landowners, Roman occupiers, the religious and political elites got rich, while the peasants lived at levels barely above subsistence.

Jesus, the peasant, was a subversive. This is evident in the company he kept, the sort he ate, drank, and socialized with, his witticisms, his violations of the purity code of his day, and especially in his stories. The parables of Jesus are stories against oppression told by one of the oppressed, directed toward the ruthless ruling class. Jesus spoke truth to power in the form of fiction, parables of peasant life, their oppression by the powerful, and how the alternate lifestyle of God's kingdom being lived out in their community could change their very existence.

Many of the parables have been interpreted allegorically, and therefore erroneously, through the years, and of all that is lost when this happens, it is what they say about power, oppression, poverty, and community that most suffers. Jesus's parables aren't about the next life, but how to live in this one.

When a landowner hires day laborers to work in his vineyard at different times throughout the day, then pays the ones who worked an hour just as much as those who worked eight, the allegorical, and I believe *mis*interpretation, has viewed the landowner as God. Because of this, his actions are seen as generous, the meaning that everyone, no matter how early or late in their lives they convert to Christianity, gets the same heavenly reward. However, when the landowner is not seen as a symbol for God, and the parable again becomes the story of a peasant speaking to power, the message and meaning are quite different. The story is then a picture of abuse and exploitation, an examination of the powerlessness of the poor, the precariousness of their position, and their systematic maltreatment by the rich.

At the end of the long, hard, hot day, the landowner had his foreman gather the workers and give them their pay, beginning with the last ones hired and moving to the first. This strange reversal and insult was their first clue that yet more abuse was headed their way. The landowner, through his foreman, demonstrates that he can do anything he wants, and there's nothing these minimum-wage day laborers can do about it. He owns them. He tells them how to line up, what their pay will be. He can make those most tired, hardest working wait the longest to receive their pittance. What can they do? But when he further disrespects and devalues them by giving the guys who worked an hour as much as he does them, one of them dares to get all Norma Rae and say something about it.

This isn't right, he says, and you know it. We've borne the burden of the work and the heat of the day, and you give those who just got here what you gave us. How can you insult and devalue us like that?

Friend, the landowner says, but it wasn't a friendly term (much like calling minimum-wage exploited workers *associates*), I'm not being unfair to you. I can do whatever I want to with *my* money. It's mine. I have the land. I have the money. I have all the power. So take your pay and get out of here! If you won't let me treat you as property and for my amusement, you're fired.

In a similar story, a man plants a vineyard, builds a wall around it, erects a watchtower, and rents it out to peasant farmers. Later, when the owner sends his servants to collect fruit from the vineyard, the peasants rise up and kill them. They do the same when the owner sends his son. What will the owner do? Jesus asks. He will come and kill them all.

Seen as an allegory, the owner is God, the son is Jesus, the peasants those who reject and kill Jesus (erroneously and dangerously seen as the Jews, adding to the horrendous history of anti-Semitism). But seen as the parable of a peasant, without being much later theologized and allegorized, Jesus's story can be seen as a picture of the powerless peasant life and a warning against violence as an answer.

Though there are many, I'll mention only one more example here.

Often seen as a story about using or losing the gifts God gives us, the parable of the minas (or talents) shows a rich nobleman about to go to a far country to be made a king calling his servants and giving them money to invest on his behalf. When he returns, the servant who had been given ten made ten more; the one who had five made five more; but the one who had been given one merely returned the one to the king, saying he knew what a hard man the nobleman was, taking out what he did not put in and reaping where he did not sow, so he buried the mina. The nobleman, now a king, takes the one mina from the servant and gives it to the one who had ten. He then has brought before him everyone who didn't want him to be king and has them killed. Are those the actions of God? Not according to Jesus, who said God is like a daddy who loves his children no matter what they do. So rather than misinterpreting this parable as an allegory, why don't we see it for what it is, a view into peasant life. If we do, we might see the king for the abusive exploiter that he is, and see the servant who removed his mina from the cycle of high-interest exploitation as the hero of the story.

The gospel of Jesus is good news for the poor. It's a vision of a community living under the reign of God, the only law, love, treating each other like family, sharing their abundance, bearing each other's burdens. This is the kingdom, hope for the poor and oppressed—not a picture of heaven, but a call to change citizenship right here and now, defect from the country of selfishness where greed is god and enter, like a child, the Kingdom of God here and now. Blessed are the poor for they have nothing to hold them back, no possessing possessions to prevent them from passing through the eye of the needle into the narrow gate.

It's What We Do

A man had two sons. He went to the first one and said, Son, go work today in the vineyard.

I can't, the first son answered, but later changed his mind and went.

Then the father went to his second son and said the same thing.

The second son said, Sure, I'd be happy to. But then he didn't go.

Which one of the two did what the father wanted?

Jesus taught that it's not what we say, but what we do that matters most. Talk is cheap. Actions are what count. Religion teaches the antithesis—it doesn't matter what you do so much as what you say, what you believe, and that you make a public profession of that belief.

Religion has become about what a person claims to believe far more than what he actually does. Fidelity to doctrine, profession of orthodoxy, not lifestyle, not actions, are what matter to religious leaders. Rather than live the radical, subversive, counter-cultural lifestyle of Jesus, we are only asked to affirm creeds the church says are correct. Because the movement was turned into a religion, it's more important to religious leaders what you believe about Christ than for you to live the way Jesus of Nazareth did.

Faith is a verb. It's something we do. It's different from mere belief, which is an emotional and intellectual assent to certain things that may or may not be true. Faith is action. They're not called acts of faith for nothing. Faithfulness is commitment, it's conduct, it's commission. We can say anything. It's what we do that matters.

Love is an active force. It flows through us, inspiring and energizing us to extend ourselves for others. It's not enough to say, I love you. In fact, if we truly love someone, we don't have to tell them, they'll know it by what we do.

Jesus said if we see someone without a coat and give them one of ours, we've loved the person, demonstrated faith. If we see someone needing food and we say to them, God bless you, or, I'll pray for you, we've acted with neither love nor faith. It's only when we feed the person that we can be said to be followers of Jesus. Notice that even the word *follower* involves action. Saying we're followers doesn't make it so—only actually following does.

The need to constantly talk about who and what we are strikes me as insecure. If we know who we are, I don't think we feel the need to constantly tell people (and perhaps ourselves). More importantly, if others can tell by how we live, who and what we are, then we don't need to tell them. Who are we trying to convince?

As the writer of the book of James said, Go ahead, try to show me your faith without works—I'll show you my faith by my works. On the witness stand, it's not what we say that matters, but what we do, what we can prove. Nearly everyone says they're innocent. We're on trial for our lives, our very souls are at stake. All

that can be considered is the evidence, only our actions can speak
for us. What do they say?

Countless people the world over are followers of Jesus, people
of the way. They may not know it—may even call themselves by
some other name. Labels aren't what matter, only actions. If they
are doing what Jesus did, what he taught, they are his followers. In
fact, according to the above story, it's far better for us to call ourselves something else entirely and do what Jesus wants us to, than
to call ourselves followers of his and not do what he said. The
authenticity and effectiveness of religion would be improved expo-
nentially if we stopped talking, stopped making claims about ourselves and our gods, and just began to do, to act, to be. Wouldn't
it be interesting if our labels were removed, our ability to run our
mouths taken from us, and others had to identify us by our actions? If we couldn't tell people who we are (or are trying to be),
what would our actions lead them to believe about us? Perhaps the
best thing we could do is close our mouths and find out.

A Settling of Accounts

A king wished to settle accounts with his servants. When he
began the accounting, there was brought to him one of the debt-
ors who owed him ten thousand talents.

Who do we identify with? Likely the servant at this point, but
the amount he owed certainly distanced him from Jesus's original
audience of peasants and common people. For the servant to have
a ten thousand talent line of credit meant he was very high up in
the hierarchy of oppression.

As he could not pay back what he owed, the master ordered
that he be sold along with his wife and children and everything
they had in order to repay the loan.

The Jewish audience hearing Jesus's story would know that the
king or master of the story is Gentile, for Jewish law forbade the
selling of a wife and children to repay debt. They would certainly
identify with the servant and see this as yet another example of
Gentile oppression and cruelty—and, of course, Jewish superiority.

Who we identify with in a story dictates the meaning of the story for us. Who has our sympathy, who we're pulling for determines how we view the tale, how we interpret what happens and how we feel about it.

Then falling down, the servant worshiped the master, saying, Have patience with me and I will repay you everything.

No Jewish servant would bow down and worship another human being, no Jewish king would want him to. This just further causes Jesus's audience to feel superior to the Gentile characters of the story.

But having pity, the master of the servant set him free and cancelled the loan for him.

Now who do we identify with? The master's mercy is unexpected. Surely we believe ourselves to be as kind and compassionate as the master of the story. We appreciate his generous act of mercy and begin to relate more with him—even as we are relieved for the servant.

And coming out of the meeting with the master, the servant found one of his fellow servants who owed him a hundred denarii. Seizing his fellow servant he nearly choked him, saying, Pay back what you owe me.

Finding out his fellow servant was unable to pay what he owed, he cast him into prison until he should repay everything.

This, too, is unexpected. How could the servant who has been forgiven so much fail to forgive so little?

Then the other servants, seeing what had happened, were deeply grieved, and coming back to their master, they told him everything that had happened.

Off stage, like us, the other servants have witnessed everything, and, like us, are outraged at their fellow servant's lack of mercy—especially after having received so much so recently himself.

Who do we identify with now? The fellow servants are us.

Then summoning the first servant, his master said to him, Evil servant, all that debt I forgave you since you begged me. And was it not necessary that you have mercy on your fellow servants as I had mercy on you? And being angry, his master handed him over to the torturers until he should pay back all that he owed.

Now instead of just going to prison until he can repay, the servant is going to be tortured—his current punishment far worse than before. And that's not all. A king has gone back on his word—actually taken back his forgiveness. Who is safe? The world is upside down. Who made everything so much worse? We did. We, as the fellow servants who, in our outrage, reported the unforgiving servant. Worst of all, we have become him. Like him, we failed to forgive. We're no different than him. Through this masterful story, Jesus causes us to do the very thing we're condemning the servant for doing.

Few film students or theologians would argue that Jesus, the storyteller, was a predecessor of Hitchcock, the director, or that the Master influenced the Master of Suspense, but in at least one instance there are some remarkable similarities. In fact, I can think of no better illustration of what Jesus did to his audience through his story than what Hitchcock did to his audience through a scene from his movie *Psycho*.

In *Psycho*, Hitchcock shows Norman Bates removing a picture of the rape of Susannah and peeping through a hole in the wall at Marion Crane as she undresses and prepares to get in the shower of her hotel room. We find his actions sick and demented and condemn him for them. Hitchcock has the camera on a side close-up shot that shows Norman's profile and the light streaming from the hole in the wall into his eye. You're sick, Norman, we think. How could you be so depraved? Then Hitch does what Jesus did. He moves the camera from the side view of Norman to shoot directly into the peephole. Norman's view becomes our view. Suddenly, we see what Norman has been seeing—and we want to, and we don't look away. We do the very thing we've been condemning Norman for. We are judged by the way we judge, measured by the measurement we use.

Jesus's original Jewish audience ultimately identified with the Gentiles of the story whom they originally felt so superior to and actually did the same thing they condemned the servant for doing. Hitchcock's Christian audience condemned Norman Bates for his actions, then proceeded to do the very thing they condemned him for. Just as you and I, through our identification with the fellow servants and through our not looking away from what we judged Norman Bates for doing, are guilty of the very same things we judged others for doing. Both Jesus and Hitchcock through master storytelling cause us to judge ourselves.

There's something inside most of us that cries out for justice. We want wrongs to be righted, good to triumph. But over and over again, Jesus exposed the hypocrisy of what we really want—which is justice for others, but mercy and understanding for ourselves. The story of the unforgiving servant shows us the absurdity and impossibility of this wish. There's either mercy for all or mercy for none. We can't withhold from others what we so desperately want for ourselves. Do unto others as you would have done unto you. With the same measurement you measure, you will be measured. Be merciful as God is merciful. Whatever is inside us that cries out for justice, that thirsts for vengeance, ceases when the person in question is us. So all we have to do is put ourselves in the other person's shoes—the very definition of compassion—become the first servant or the one he refused to forgive instead of the fellow servants on the sideline feeling so superior, and we won't be so quick to settle accounts any more.

The Kingdom of God is a Party

In sharp contrast to the formal, buttoned-up, often austere synagogue of Jesus's day and the religious centers of our own, Jesus communicated and demonstrated that what the Kingdom of God is most like is a party.

The Kingdom of God is a giant, festive party with great food, good wine, old friends, warmth, music—that everyone is invited to.

Jesus's vision of the ultimate expression of a gathering of God is a party that wouldn't be complete, wouldn't be right, just wouldn't be the same, without you. It's God's party and she wants you there.

When the prodigal son comes home, what does Jesus say his dad does? Throws a party. I had to celebrate, he explains to his other son who doesn't understand and thinks a party is the last thing his brother deserves. My son was lost and now is found, was dead and is now alive.

God is a party-giver, a father who likes having his children and their friends surrounding him, having a good time.

Unlike most parties, where a limited number of people are invited, everyone is welcome in the Kingdom of God. There's nothing exclusive about the gathering of God, the table of the Lord. Contrary to what you've been told, you don't have to do certain things to earn an invitation to this party. It's not who you know or what you do or how much you have. And you're not just welcome, but wanted.

If God's party is poorly attended, it's not because God doesn't want everyone there. On the contrary. God wants us to attend far more than we even want to. Jesus opens his arms to all and invites us to the abundant life-of-the-party lifestyle. It's not God who keeps us from partying, but us. God doesn't reject us. We reject God. The party is thrown, all things are ready. If we don't rush in and get our groove on, it's because we either don't want to or have listened to the lies of loveless, humorless party crashers.

A man of great wealth was having a party. In the customary way of the time and culture, he invited everyone, telling them the approximate time—what we would call today a save-the-date notice. Then, when all things were prepared, he sent out his workers to tell everyone, Come, for all things are ready.

The workers did as they were instructed, but the people they spoke to began to make excuses for why they couldn't make it. One dude said he had invested in some real estate and had to go take a look at it. Another guy said he had just bought a new Mustang and had to take it out and let the ponies run. One lady said she had another party to go to—sorry, but she just couldn't be in two places at once.

Of course, the excuses are just that. They have no merit, no basis in reality. No real estate investor would buy a piece of property sight unseen, no one would buy a Mustang without taking a

test drive first, and there would be no other parties going on during the same time as this one—there's not a soul in the village who
would be so disrespectful and inconsiderate as to throw a party
during the same time as one of her neighbors. It doesn't matter
what excuse they gave, a no is a no. Rejection is still rejection, no
matter how you package it. The girl who tells the guy, It's not you,
it's me, and the guy who tells the girl, You're a great friend, but I
just don't think of you in that way, are still saying no even if it's
more of a no thank you.

Why don't we want to go to God's party? Maybe we think it'll
be a drag—like the difference in going to a party with our friends
versus going to a party with our parents. Maybe it's because of
who's going to be there. Maybe we really don't like the idea that
everyone is invited. We'd be more comfortable at a more exclusive
party of people who are more like us. Maybe we really don't believe it's a party. Unlike the workers of the story, religious leaders and authority figures don't tell us about the party. They don't
extend the invitation so we don't even know it's going on. Or they
tell us it's not really a party, but something else—like a boring service for saints instead of a fun party for sinners.

Jesus spent his life partying, surrounded by people who knew
how to have a good time, who enjoyed eating and drinking and
being together. He was called a drunk and a slut and he said that's
what God's Kingdom is like. No wonder they killed him.

You're invited to the biggest, best, longest-running party in
history. You are an honored guest. Relax, recline, you're among
friends—people who genuinely love you. This gathering is about
celebration, connection, enjoying the host's warmth and generosity, about feeling at home and having a good time. God wants us
to celebrate the incontrovertible, undeniable fact that we are loved
and cherished beyond all reason, that we belong, that we are val-

ued. There's no better reason for a party, there's no greater cause for celebration.

The Subversive Sage

If the Kingdom of God is not of this world, is, in fact, opposite in nearly every way, it follows that the wisdom of Jesus would seem like foolishness. So absurd were his assertions, that his own family thought he'd lost his mind. So contrary and counter-cultural were his teachings, that the orthodox religious leaders believed he was possessed by a demon.

Of the two broad categories of wisdom teachers—those who affirm their culture by expounding conventional wisdom and those who attack their culture by sharing subversive, counter-cultural wisdom—Jesus was clearly the latter. Rather than applying his imagination and wit in the service of the collected and excepted wisdom of his time, the words breathed by Jesus demonstrated the limits of logic and revealed the shortcomings of people's perceived, popular assumptions.

The difference between conventional wisdom and the alternative wisdom of Jesus can be heard in his expression, You have heard of old . . . but I say unto you . . .

Today, those who call themselves by his name have gone back
to what was said of old. We have at best incorporated Jesus's
radical, subversive wisdom into conventional wisdom, watering it
down so much it's no longer recognizable, and at worst completely
ignored the unselfish vision of life that asks so much of us.

We've also lost Jesus's wit, sarcasm, and insightful humor.
Partly, it's lost in translation. Two thousand years and a nearly
unrecognizable culture separating us, we read right over it, making
the once shocking and scandalous, simplistic and sweet; the bit-
ing and barbed, benign and banal. We've lost the poignancy of his
pithy sayings, the affect of his aphorisms.

We've heard them so many times, we no longer hear them: It's
easier for a camel to go through the eye of a needle than for a rich man to
enter the Kingdom of God. Why do you focus on the speck of sawdust
in your brother's eye and ignore the huge plank in your own? You are the
salt of the earth, but if the salt loses its flavor, how will it get it back? Wide
is the gate and broad is the way that leads to destruction, but small is the
gate and narrow is the road that leads to life. You are the light of the world.
People don't light a lamp and stick it under a bowl. Don't worry—who of
you can by worrying can add a single hour to your life? Don't give what is
sacred to swine. Let the dead bury the dead. Unless you become like a little
child, you will not enter the Kingdom of God.

There are many, many others, including stories, such as the
widow who pesters a judge so much he finally gives her justice
and the friend who shows up in the middle of the night needing a
place to stay.

In the Kingdom of God, the last shall be first; the poor, rich;
the lost, found; the least, greatest. According to Jesus, the poor,
brokenhearted, hungry, and persecuted should be happy and the
meek, merciful, peacemakers will be the children of God and
inherit the earth. In Jesus's kingdom, love is all. We should love
everyone, including the most unlovable—even our enemies, even

our oppressors and persecutors, actually turning the other cheek when we are struck. We should share all that we have, give gladly to those in need. Think about it. It's absurd—so naive as to be dangerous. What kind of fool doesn't look out for himself? What kind of benighted simpleton loves his abuser?

Behold the man! He's sad, really, abandoned, beaten, made a fool. He is powerless. His captors have mockingly placed a make-shift robe on him and a crown fashioned from thorns. King? Of what? Who would follow such a weak and defeated king? Who would be so foolish?

By ignoring or changing or domesticating this aspect of the gospel, we have failed to be fools. Unlike the king we claim to follow, we clutch at wealth, grasp for power. We seek strength, refuse to willingly be weak.

By all worldly measurements, Jesus was a fool, a naive dreamer who was shown what happens to those who dare to challenge the way the world works. God's holy fool calls to us. Come be foolish with me, he says. Dare to dream, to believe that insanity is sanity, foolishness is wisdom. We can't have it both ways. We can't be wise according to this world and follow the subversive sage. If Jesus was right, then foolishness is the truest wisdom, weakness the greatest strength, the vulnerability of love the most powerful force. No wonder his family and community thought he was insane. If we follow him into madness, will ours think any differently of us?

Christ and Culture

Separating Christ from culture—both his and our own—is essential to truly following him. The failure to do so leads to absurdity, irrelevance, and idolatry.

To properly understand Jesus, his message and meaning, we must understand the cultural context in which he lived. Only after viewing him in context can we ever hope to lift his teachings from his culture and apply them to our lives. We must also know the differences between his and our own culture—our social and cultural norms and traditions—and be able to keep them separate from transcendent truth.

If we fail to separate Jesus from his culture, we move backward into, among other things, ignorance, superstition, and empty rituals. As we continue to develop and evolve, we learn more about ourselves and the universe—far more than anyone in the first century even dreamed of—and the only way Jesus's teachings can be applied to contemporary life and all its implications is if we separate his teachings from his time and place and apply those truths and principles to our own.

The reason so many religious people seem ignorant and backward is because of their attempt to apply a two-thousand-year-old culture to the way they live today. They are literally backward—living two thousand years in the past. They're living a male-dominated, hierarchical culture that was largely uneducated, where slavery was a part of everyday life, where women had no rights and were considered property, where options were severely limited, life was short, and kings and priests ruled.

Since Jesus was so counter-cultural, most of the culture we receive with anything that also carries pieces of his message comes from other biblical writers—and it's the very cultural conventions Jesus stood against.

Jesus was Jewish. He lived in first century Palestine. If we are to understand him, his message, his actions, we have to understand the cultural context in which he existed.

There's nothing sacred about culture. There's no reason for us to adopt his culture. We have to remove him from it as best we can—which we can only do once we understand it.

Jesus continually criticized and corrected culture—specifically the religion and politics—of his day. You have heard it said, but I say unto you, he would often say, offering a new way to see God, religion, the world, and society—one that was far more faithful to the nature and character of God. Like our own, the culture, religion, political power, and social structures of his day were corrupt.

Today most people seem to be following the culture, religion, and politics Jesus was trying to correct instead of his revolution—his revision of his culture. How tragic is it that people bearing the name of Jesus practice the type of culture, politics, and religion that he railed against, that he said was based on a misunderstanding of God.

Not only do we have to resist the temptation to hallow Jesus's culture, adopting it along with his teachings, but we must also resist the urge to view our own as sacred and inseparable from the good news of the Kingdom. Failure to do so leads to an arrogant and ignorant self-righteousness that views our nation as blessed and approved by God, erroneously elevating our culture while also diluting the timeless truths of the way.

The process of separating kernels of truth from the husk of culture isn't easy. It's also never ending. We must continually and critically examine culture—both Jesus's and ours—with eyes open to see and ears open to hear and hearts and minds committed to truth above all else. Only then can we be faithful to the Kingdom of God, not merely puppets of our own culture, but transcending it to walk in the sublime, divine, upside-down Kingdom so different from any we could create.

Growing Down

When Jesus said unless we become like little children we would never enter the Kingdom of God, he wasn't doing so out of sentimentality or a Pollyanna perception of children or childhood. Who better than Mary's little bastard to know how painful childhood could be?

Children aren't any more inherently innocent or good than adults. In fact, children can be extremely cruel, the playground more potentially damaging than the battleground. The taunts of children can wound the soul, skewer self-esteem, damage a person's self-perception for life.

Ask anyone who works with children, or better yet, ask any child, if children are more caring or more kind than their adult counterparts. They are not. After all, what are adults, but bigger, more experienced children?

So what did Jesus mean? Why do we have to change? What is it about little children we are to become like?

Little children are open.

They've yet to be hardened and closed by experience and education. Unlike many adults, they know how little they know. They don't have answers, they have questions. Their sponge-like receptivity means they soak up everything around them. Willing to try new and different things, continually seeking new experiences, children are open to the magnificent and mysterious universe in ways that cause them to benefit from every moment.

Jesus said when a farmer plants his seed, the condition of the soil determines the quality of the crop. Compact soil, trodden by traffic, hardened by pelting rain and baking sun won't allow the seed to penetrate, but good, soft, loose soil is open and receptive to the seed and produces a great crop. Children lack the hardness and defensiveness many adults have acquired over the years and, therefore, are open to the seeds of life.

Little children are curious.

They still thirst for knowledge, their questions endless, their appetites insatiable. Unlike most adults, children aren't under the illusion that they know much of anything. They want to know, know they don't know, and are unafraid to ask. Little children live with an awe and wonder many adults have long since lost.

Little children are imaginative.

Perhaps the most powerful gift God has given us, our imaginations, have the ability to solve all problems and create a far better world. Imagination is where everything begins. We have to imagine a thing before we can make it so. Einstein said that imagination was more important than knowledge. It's more important, more foundational, than anything. The difference between little children and many adults is that little children use their imaginations. Jesus used his imagination to envision the Kingdom of God as a present reality in us and among us, and in doing so imagined the best possible world, one we could live in if only we, too, could imagine it.

It is in and through the imagination that we access and connect with the divine, with the ineffable, the transcendent, the ultimate reality.

To change and become like little children means we must dust off our imaginations and begin to use them again. Fantasize, daydream, envision, pretend, make believe, imagine. Our access to God is largely through our imaginations.

Little children are teachable.

Because of their openness and curiosity, because of their lack of pride and ego, children are continually learning. Still forming, little children are malleable, eager for experience, readily receptive. Why do we think we're formed? How can we be satisfied knowing so little? Unlike their adult counterparts, children are willing to learn from anyone and anything—regardless of credentials, education, medium, or venue. When we limit our learning to certain people, places, or packages, we lose our child-like teachability and do just that—limit ourselves.

Little children are forgiving.

As cruel and unkind as children can be, they are also very quick to forgive, and rarely hold a grudge for long. Children don't walk around with the weight of negative emotions and resentments that adults do, because instead of nursing insults and injuries they let go of them. Our adult egos will destroy us if we let them. If we don't, like little children, forgive those who have hurt us, we will never heal, but be the walking wounded, weighed down by the debt we feel we're owed or distracted from life by thoughts of redress and retribution.

Little children are playful.

True holiness is playful, true righteousness fun. The freedom of childhood allows for a lighthearted, humorous approach to life, a carefree abandon that finds fun in all things. We must change and become like little children, trust our father and mother in heaven and play the holy fool. Playing puts things in perspective, laughing at ourselves, not taking ourselves too seriously, enabling us to enjoy our lives while being more productive.

Children are creative.

Except for acting compassionately, we are never more like God than when we are creative. Children live creatively. Creativity is not something they do occasionally. It's their approach to life. The creative life is the soulful approach to every aspect of existence— from the mundane and potentially monotonous to the exciting and extraordinary. Children don't have to be accomplished artists to have artistic lives. Children don't have to be poets to live poetically. Being creative is as simple as following the lead of your soul, being true to your truest self the way children are.

Creativity doesn't require originality so much as an original approach. I think many people feel that in order to be creative or artistic they have to come up with something original. There probably really is nothing new under the sun, but our own unique approach can breathe new life into anything we attempt.

The child-like creative life is the life we were meant to live. It's the one in which we are most ourselves because we're listening to our hearts, following the lead of our souls, doing things in our own unique way. Being creative is as simple and as complex as being ourselves.

Children are present.

Perhaps because they have so little past and because they have so much future, little children take the time and attention to be fully present in the present moment. Their focus is so intense they often lose track of time and any awareness of what's going on around them. In doing so, they get the most out of life.

The present moment is all we have. The past is gone. The future never gets here. This moment, right now, is all there is. Like children, we must be fully engaged, completely present, letting go of the past, not worrying about the future. If not, the past and future will rob us of our lives, stealing moment after moment.

There is a child within you, one you know well. You are that child. The little child you were still resides deep inside you. You got bigger, you've had more experiences, but you, the child you, are still inside. Perhaps that's what Jesus meant when he said the Kingdom of God is within you. You can change, become like a little child, and enter the Kingdom of God. Look within. Find the little you there and become him or her again. Open yourself up, unleash your curiosity, reignite your imagination, play and create and be fully present in the present. Grow down instead of up.

The Jewish Jesus

In one sense, there are an infinite number of Jesuses. From the historical Jesus to the Christ of faith to the personalized and individualized Jesus of billions, no other figure in human history has been more acquisitioned and altered, adopted and assumed. Inevitable as this is, there really is only one Jesus, and he was Jewish.

Perhaps what has been lost more than anything else since the Gentile hijacking of Jesus is his Jewishness. Jesus was a Jew—racially, religiously, culturally, politically a Jew. And though he transcends all these things, he cannot be fully understood without understanding his Jewishness, without understanding his Judaism.

Jesus practiced Judaism, the religion of his people, his religion. Though he challenged the religious leaders and elites of his day, he was not critical of Judaism, but of the ways in which they had strayed from it. In fact, the entirety of Jesus's message and ministry can been seen as a call to return to the true heart of Judaism. Jesus lived and died as a Jew. Maybe he was resurrected a Gentile, a cosmic Christ, but he remains Jewish—and to lose that is to lose him. As people as diverse as Nietzsche and Mark Twain have so insightfully put it, there's only ever been one Christian and he was Jewish.

Nearly all of Jesus's early followers were Jewish. The Jesus movement or the way was Jewish. Had Jesus's Jewish followers not been faithful to him and his teachings, no one reading this would have ever even heard of Jesus.

Because Jesus, as a good Jewish rabbi, was constantly debating other Jews about the true heart of their religion and because a movement formed around him, his vision for the future of Judaism was in competition with other Jewish sects of his time—the Pharisees, Sadducees, Essenes, etc. This debate intensified as the Gospels were being written and the temple was being destroyed. In the Gospels and Christian Scriptures, especially in the hands of the growing Gentile population of the church, this competition, written in such a way as to blame the Jews for rejecting and executing Jesus, became anti-Judaism and eventually began to morph into anti-Semitism. What began as a kind of sibling rivalry among Jews turned deadly when taken up by the Roman Empire—the very entity that actually was responsible for executing Jesus. The Jews (as it is written mainly but not exclusively in the Gospel of John), have been erroneously blamed for deicide and persecuted because of it. How tragically ironic. It'd be comical if it weren't so insidious and lethal. Jesus, the Jewish rabbi, his life, message, and meaning, have been used to justify anti-Semitism.

Like all of the great spiritual teachers, and I think he's the single greatest, Jesus transcends religion. Truth needs no label. Love is universal. I, as an American living in the early twenty-first century, am truly grateful that the Jesus movement didn't remain only a reform movement within Judaism, but I also know that to truly understand the movement and the man behind it, I have to respect and appreciate Judaism, who, after all, gave us Jesus. Without Judaism there would be no Jesus.

Context is all. Jesus can no more be truly or fully understood apart from Judaism than the Christian Scriptures can be understood separate from the Hebrew Scriptures. Lift Jesus out of his cultural and religious context and he and his message are altered, changed, at best incomplete. You don't have to practice Judaism to follow Jesus, but you have to comprehend Judaism to comprehend Jesus—and that can't begin with a bias against Judaism.

The individual voice can become the communal voice, the regional voice, the universal, but only when they remain in the context of their region, of their community. It's one of the most ironic things I've learned from being a fiction writer. The more individual, the more specific a person or detail is located in its own context, the more universal it becomes. Jesus can only be the cosmic Christ when he is simultaneously seen as a first-century Jewish peasant and rabbi. His message can only be as meaningful and universal as it is Jewish—individually, communally, regionally Jewish.

Family Values

Often used by Fundamentalists and politicians as a poster child for family values, Jesus is anything but. Born without a father at a time when legitimacy was everything, Mary's little bastard had a radical idea about who his family really was.

While teaching in a house full of people, someone came up to Jesus and said, Your family's outside looking for you.

No, Jesus responded, my family is inside here with me, looking for God.

His mother and brothers had come to Baker Act him, to take him back home and get him some help. They were convinced he was out of his mind. Ah, family. Warms the heart, doesn't it?

Jesus's relationship with his family seems as challenging as the rest of ours are. An absent father, a controlling mother, brothers who thought his fame had gone to his head, Jesus formed a new family—one where God is father and mother and all fellow human beings are brothers and sisters.

Mary, like many mothers, seems to have had her own agenda for her son, and her attempts to direct his path, change his course, were met with resistance and rebuke. And from every indication, Jesus's relationship with Joseph was nonexistent.

Call no man on earth father, Jesus said. You have one father and he is in heaven. When you pray, say, Our dad in heaven . . .

Would Jesus have had such an intimate and radical relationship with his abba if he had had an earthly father? Perhaps, but like him, all of us can learn from our family dynamics and experiences. We can see family as the metaphor for God and our relationships even as our own family fails to embody the best of what family should be.

Once when a potential follower of Jesus's asked to go back and bury his father before joining him, Jesus said, Let the dead bury the dead. No one fit for the Kingdom puts his hand to the plow then looks back.

As troublesome as all of this is, it gets worse:

If anyone comes to me and does not hate his mother and father, his wife and children, brothers and sisters, even his own life, he cannot be my disciple, for I have come to turn a man against his father, a daughter against her mother. A person's enemies will be those of his own household.

Of course, Jesus taught we are to love our enemies—even when they come from our own household, and hate here is a comparative word. Love itself can seem like hate when compared to such a great, incomparable love. Jesus didn't teach to hate, and we can't use his family experiences or teachings to justify our animosity and unforgiveness toward any member of our family, but the fact remains, Jesus had family troubles and understands ours.

Jesus's relationship with his family was complicated. Whose isn't? Without advocating abandoning our families or alleviating our responsibilities toward them, Jesus taught and lived that true

family isn't as much about birth and blood as direction and deci-
sion. Jesus doesn't narrow the definition of family. He expands it.
All of humanity is our family, and the family we're the closest to is
the one we choose and who chooses us—nothing's to say this can't
be those who give us birth and share our blood, but nothing's to
say it has to be either.

Unto Us

In a cold, dark cave in the middle of nowhere, Jesus was born the way all humans are—and it involved blood and pain and private parts. Unlike Moses, the Prince of Egypt, or Abraham, a Prince of Ur, or Prince Siddhartha, Jesus entered this world in the lowliest of ways—amid rumor and scandal, to a young peasant girl pregnant out of wedlock—to be shunned as illegitimate in the small town where he grew up known as Mary's little bastard.

And we've lost this.

We've cleaned it up, domesticated it, turned it into a Hallmark-sponsored movie of the week. We've thrown in some angels and shepherds and wise men, left out certain details of natural child-birth in general and the specifics of this one in particular, and let some kids act it out in a nice, clean-carpeted place of worship, and it's an act of betrayal.

Scholars question how much of the nativity story is histori-cal—and not without good reason. Pregnant virgins, guiding stars, angelic choirs, magicians from the East are all the stuff of legends

far older than Christianity. Thankfully, truth is not predicated on
history. And what could be more true in its essence than God being born in a barn? The story of the birth of Jesus is the paradox
of humanity. The creative, spiritual force behind all that is incar-
nating himself into the dirty, dying body of an animal is surprising
only when we forget what we are—the contradictory elements
of dust of the earth and breath of God. Who better to speak to
creatures who are paradoxically lowly dirt and lofty spirit than a
God who gets shat out by a poor, unwed teen mother to live the
obscure little life of a peasant and die strung up, spread out naked
on a cross for the whole world to see?

When we forget about these things, when we try to make Jesus
respectable, we lose something precious, profound, and powerful.
When we lose our bastard messiah, our wounded healer, our peasant prince, we lose the gospel for the poor, the counter-cultural
power of love. Perhaps the second worst thing to ever happen
to the message of Jesus was it becoming the official, approved
religion of Rome (the first was so much being added to it and it
becoming a religion at all). Power and status can't coexist with the
true, scandalous fringe movement of compassion and justice.

The Puritanical, holiness, repressed strain of self-righteous
preening and posing that has become so much of Christianity is an
unequivocal betrayal of Jesus.

There's nothing clean about Jesus or his followers. Jesus
spent his life attacking the purity system, taking on the fakers and
pretenders, the dishonest posers who claimed to be clean while
everyone else was dirty. He rejected the distinctions of clean and
unclean. He hung out with the dirty people, spread a table at which
everyone was welcomed, attended parties so much he was known
as a drunk and a whoremonger. Everything is clean and unclean,
pure and impure.

The story of Jesus is a dirty, filthy affair that I wouldn't want to clean up if I could. From its humble beginnings to its scandalous development and spread among the drunk-ass poor and disease-ridden whores, this good news for the oppressed and marginalized is at its best when it's at its most fringe, counter-cultural, unsentimental, and downright dirty. Lose the respectability, quit pretending, stop posing. Have nothing to do with the repressed, bloodless, clean, upright citizens running the current sham, and hang instead with Mary's little bastard and his friends—real, earthy, fallible, filthy sinners who are not ashamed of their manger messiah, who can relate to humble beginnings, and who are comfortable in barns and bars and houses of ill repute.

The Company We Keep

We are known by the company we keep. Who we hang with and who we won't reveals as much about us as anything else. The righteous hang with other righteous, but true saints (who are also the best sinners) hang with sinners.

Jesus was often criticized because of the company he kept. He was known as a drunk, a pimp, a glutton, a friend of sinful and impure people.

The purity system of Jesus's day dominated every aspect of public life. Who and what was clean and unclean, pure and impure, approved and disapproved was used to separate and oppress people. Jesus spent his time with people who were unclean and impure, doing things that were disapproved of. Through his teachings and his lifestyle, Jesus waged a full-on assault on the purity system, exposing its shallowness, hypocrisy, paranoia, and false morality.

Under the purity system, one of the chief ways to stay pure was to avoid impure people. If you could be defiled by the company you kept, then you best stay among the righteous. Jesus did anything but. Not only did Jesus have a bad reputation, but nearly everything he did was scandalous. Subverting all the social niceties and norms of his day, Jesus constantly shocked and offended those around him.

Like the Pharisaical piety of Jesus's day, the Puritanical undercurrent running through the culture of our own causes anyone who truly follows Jesus to be counter-cultural, rebellious, out of sync, out of step with the mainstream, weird, unpatriotic, liberal, socialist, bleeding-heart, sinful. Religious leaders of our day have far more in common with Jesus's critics than Jesus.

To the extent that many modern religious people have any interaction at all with sinners (as they define them, which usually means aren't like them), it's infrequent and only as a ministry—an act of charity from a position of superiority. This was not the case with Jesus. Sinners, the sick, the poor, the impure and unclean (as defined by the purity system) weren't just ministry for Jesus. They were his friends, his people, who he preferred to live with. Mary's little bastard was far more comfortable with foulmouthed fishermen and working women than the devout of his day.

In addition to constantly communicating God's unbiased and unconditional love, Jesus continually demonstrated it in two powerful ways—open-table fellowship and healing the sick.

Sharing a meal with someone in Jesus's time and culture was an extremely intimate act. Only sex was considered more intimate. Jesus didn't just go near impure people, he was intimate with them. Everyone was welcome at his table—hookers, pimps, drunks, drug addicts, half-breeds, the sick and dying, traitors. Everyone.

Jesus's open-table fellowship was an open attack on the purity system, offering an alternative vision of the Kingdom of God—an inclusive community where categories of clean and unclean, pure and impure, righteous and unrighteous are nonexistent. And these weren't just any meals, they were celebrations. Jesus is described as reclining with the outcasts at these meals, which means they were festive occasions (they sat up at ordinary meals and reclined at celebrations). Jesus didn't just eat with the impure, he partied with them. In Jesus's alternative vision, the Kingdom of God is a party where everyone is invited.

The open-table fellowship Jesus began continued after his death. Jesus's first followers had the table as the center of their gatherings. Communion for them was a meal where everyone was welcome. People shared what they had, little as it was, with everyone else, and everyone shared in the love and acceptance of God. How different this is from the formal ritual of communion today where what is served is tepid grape juice and a morsel of Styrofoam-like wafer or a crumb of bread, and those served are approved members certified as pure by the institution because of what they profess to believe.

Jesus also attacked the purity system through his practices as a healer. The sick and maimed were seen as unclean, impure. Sin was suspected as the cause for their infirmities. They were viewed as cursed by God because of something they or their parents had done. By touching bleeding women, blind men, and people with leprosy, Jesus demonstrated God's unconditional love. He risked his life to show they weren't untouchables or outcasts, but precious to God.

By eating with sinners and touching the diseased, he demonstrated that true religion is compassion. It's about caring for one another. It's about being pure of heart, not social standing, occupation, or the appearance of wholeness. Placing people before principles and purity, Jesus attacked a religion that had lost its humanity, had lost its soul. We must do the same—even though some religions now bear his name. We must reject the religion that has rejected Jesus, his humanity and his revolutionary revision, in favor of the way, a lifestyle that puts people first, sees them not merely as souls to be saved, but precious, loved, and accepted by God. Like us, they, too, hunger for acceptance and connection, to be touched and held and healed by shared meals that feed the body even as they nourish the soul.

Things Left Unsaid

What is left unsaid is nearly as important as what is said. The white space on a page of text or the silence in between the notes that are played shape the work, define it, and give it meaning. It is as instructive for us to consider what Jesus didn't say nearly as much as what he did.

From the very beginning of the Jesus Movement, people have overemphasized and de-emphasized things that Jesus said and did. Each of us attaches importance, meaning, and emphasis to that which most resonates with us or that we most need, often ignoring or downplaying everything else. This seems far more benign to me than actually attributing words to Jesus he never spoke. The writers of the Gospels did it, the author of John by far the greatest offender, but we continue to do it. The most common practice is taking other words found in the Bible and giving them the same weight and importance as Jesus's or acting as if he said them.

I'm not arguing against logical inferences drawn from what Jesus said or did not say, did or did not do. I also realize that because of the difference in time and culture, we have to lift principles from what Jesus said in order to apply them to the context of our lives. However, we should make sure the inferences and principles are actually taken from Jesus, his core teachings, his essential message.

Jesus didn't say a single word about church attendance. It's not surprising that the church attendees equate church attendance with righteousness. After all, their leaders, who have a vested interest in their attendance, have convinced them of it. However, to act as if it's what Jesus would do, when he spent very little time in synagogue and reserved his harshest criticisms for organized religion, is deceitful and disingenuous. To the extent that the religion of today resembles that of Jesus's, a person of the way should be in conflict with it, not part of it.

Jesus never uttered a single syllable about homosexuality. Other writers in the Bible did, though not often—there are less than a handful of references about homosexuality in the entire Bible. But Jesus never said anything about homosexuality.

Jesus never said anything about abortion, family values.

Jesus never said anything about dress, makeup, or hairstyles. Jesus's attack on outward religiosity and the purity system, his association with hookers and drunks, is in direct opposition to the Puritanical, conservative, and holiness strain of prudishness.

Jesus never taught on the importance of tradition or patriotism or democracy or capitalism.

Jesus never told people if they didn't accept him as their personal savior that they would burn in hell for all eternity. His biographers, interpreters, and evangelists have, but he didn't. Christianity, its art, creeds, and worship practices, emphasizes Jesus's birth and death, skipping from born unto the virgin Mary . . . to suffered under Pontius Pilate. Viewing Jesus's life and death purely under the rubric of ancient Israel's sacrificial system makes

Jesus our sin offering and high priest and alleviates us of all responsibility. Jesus's life—what he said and what he did—is what matters most, is our example of how to live (loving our neighbors as ourselves), how to relate to God (as our abba, not an angry god craving blood sacrifice). Many people within the religion claiming to follow Jesus largely ignore his life because they don't want to live it, and they are taught that the suffering, sacrifice, and death of Jesus means they don't have to suffer, sacrifice, or die.

Jesus never taught that God helps those who help themselves. On the contrary, Jesus said that God helps those who *can't* help themselves—and the way he does it is through us, which he can't do if we're too busy helping ourselves.

Jesus not only remained silent on many subjects, but he also experienced the silence of God. In the way that what is left unsaid underscores and defines what is said, it is God's absence that makes his presence all the more precious, her silence that gives meaning to her words when she does speak.

It's late. Jesus is alone, forsaken by his friends when he needs them most. The garden, known as the place of crushing, is quiet, the winepress still, the only sounds those of Jesus begging for his life. But not all Jesus's prayers were answered. The plea of, Daddy, please let this cup pass from me, and the silence that followed, continues to give solace to those whose prayers continue to go unanswered.

Stripped, beaten, humiliated, hanging on a cross like a common criminal in unbearable pain, Jesus asks why, and the haunting, My God, my God, why have you forsaken me, the last words he ever spoke, reverberate throughout all human history, its echo encouraging all who hear the nothing to their questions. Of course, it's not nothing, is it? It's something. It's silence, and silence isn't merely the absence of sound but a humbling, haunting answer all its own.

Listen! Do you hear it? It's not just the absence of sound, but the sound of silence. Jesus is the word God has spoken. Hear him. When he is silent, resist the urge to fill the void with other words, remain silent, as well. Certain things are best left unsaid. In the beginning was the word . . . Before the beginning was the silence.

The Power and the Glory

He stands naked and powerless, a single peasant against the entire Roman Empire. It's nearly comical. Nearly. He is a king without a kingdom, without an army, without a prayer. He has been brought before a representative of the most powerful empire the world has ever known.

You are the king of the Jews? Pilate asks. *You*? Is this is a joke? Surely somebody's trying to pull one over on me. This pathetic creature can't be the king of anything.

When is a king not a king? When is a kingdom not a kingdom? My kingdom is not of this world, Jesus says.

What does that mean? Is the Kingdom of God purely spiritual? Is it only futuristic? Apocalyptic? If so, why the conflict?

Why even call it a kingdom? The moment Jesus uses the term kingdom to describe the conditions in which his father's will is done, it immediately brings the kingdom and him into conflict with the kings and kingdoms of this world.

How can a king whose kingdom is not of this world be executed as a political prisoner by the Roman Empire?

Though not of this world, Jesus's kingdom is obviously a
threat to the kingdoms of this world.

With statements like, My kingdom is not of this world, Render
unto Caesar what is Caesar's and unto God what is God's, and,
The Kingdom of God doesn't come with your careful observation, nor will people say Here it is or There it is because the Kingdom of God is within you, Jesus avoids politics and the grasping
of temporal political power with the same tenacity so many of his
followers pursue it today.

But does this mean Jesus wasn't political?
Jesus wasn't political in that he wasn't involved in politics, didn't
use political systems; however, nearly everything he said and did
had political implications. He was called a king. He continually
spoke about his father's kingdom. He was executed as a political
prisoner.

How does a spiritual kingdom threaten the kingdoms of this
world?

Though not of this world, the Kingdom of God is in the
world, influencing, challenging, changing the people of the world,
calling them out of other kingdoms and into the unkingdom. The
Kingdom of God is an alternative, a reality where God's will is
done—a dimension of peace, justice, community, and love. In this
kingdom, leaders serve, widows and orphans are cared for, the
haves share with the have-nots, people extend themselves on behalf of others, they care and share. They are open and honest and
like children.

Jesus never entered into the political process, never attempted
to rule—just the opposite, in fact. Yet he, the uncrowned king,
and his unseen kingdom, posed a threat to the kingdoms of this

world. Why? Precisely because he wasn't involved in politics, never accepted a position of power. By remaining outside the political process, by being objective, by not using temporal human power, by not aligning himself with a party or platform, Jesus was able to speak out against injustice, inequity, and iniquity.

Tragically, this is a lesson too many of Jesus's followers haven't learned. History is a narrative whose arc is the pursuit of power—something religious people do as much or more as nonreligious.

Like his followers today, Jesus's first followers lusted after power and place, misunderstanding Jesus like so many have continued to do. When James and John asked to sit at his left and right in his kingdom, the other disciples grew angry and became indignant. Jesus's response is a message we desperately need to be reminded of today: You know that the rulers of the Gentiles lord it over them and their high officials exercise authority over them. Not so with you. Instead, whoever wants to become great among you must be your servant, and whoever wants to be first must be slave of all. For even the son of man did not come to be served, but to serve.

Jesus understood what so many of those who bear his name in vain do not. You can't be a prophet and a politician. By prophet I simply mean one who speaks out against corruption, injustice, and oppression—even when it's being done by his or her own country. In the tradition of the great prophets of Israel, we must remain separate from politics and the seat of power. The reason Samuel could rebuke Saul, or Nathan, David, was because they weren't seduced by power and money, but remained true to their calling.

The Kingdom of God ceases to be a threat to the kingdoms of this world when it becomes one of them—or at least part of them. Of course, it ceases to be the Kingdom of God at that point also. How can we speak truth to power when we *are* the power? How can we have any objectivity if we are part of the system of injustice and oppression?

When followers of Jesus align themselves with power, when they become traditionally political, they are no longer following Jesus or representing his kingdom.

Empire is against the Kingdom of God—whether it's Rome or Spain or Europe or America. To be a part of it, however unwittingly, is to be against the kingdom.

Did Christianity eventually conquer the Roman Empire? Or was it the other way around? Rome executed Jesus only to have Christianity become the official religion of the empire a few hundred years later. But was that a victory? For Christianity, maybe, but for Jesus, his movement, and the Kingdom of God? What emerged from the joining of the politics of Rome and the religion of a small Jewish sect taken over by Gentile converts became known as Christianity and it spread around the world, but is it still a kingdom not of this world?

Power corrupts, which is why Jesus refused it—something many of his followers have yet to follow him in. The offspring of the unholy union between empire and religion is too compromised, too contaminated, too changed to resemble the powerless peasant standing bruised and bloodied before Pilate.

Like so many empires of the past, many today see their nation-empire as the New Jerusalem, believing themselves to have a divine destiny. And like so many of the empowered of the past, they live with a sense of entitlement, righteousness, and supremacy. A person with power is dangerous, a person with power and the belief that God is on his side and that he's on a special mission is far more so.

Instead of living the life of the kingdom and offering an alternative, far too many calling themselves followers of Jesus are fighting culture wars, involved in corrupt politics, deception, schemes, and generally working through and according to the kingdoms of this world to establish a theocracy where their god rules through them. This form of religion and politics is the dominant force of our time.

Jesus said the Kingdom of God is not of this world, that it doesn't operate the way the kingdoms of the world do. So no matter how loudly certain people profess to be following Jesus, if they conduct themselves in the same manner as the kingdoms of this world—use the same tactics, fight for power the same way—they are no longer aligned with the kingdom that is not according to this world, but with those aligned against it.

The Gospel According to Jesus

The Good News isn't just good—it's the best news ever. It's shockingly good, and it is this: God is love.

You have heard it said of old that God is a distant deity, angry and vengeful, Jesus said, but I say that God is actually a loving, patient parent who loves you so much you can risk loving others. God is love. That's his nature, character, being. God is like a kind father who cares and provides for his children, a tenderhearted mother who feels what her children are feeling, aches in her womb when they ache. God is a father who is patient with his children, who loves them even when they do wrong. God is like a mother hen whose greatest joy is caring for her chicks, gathering them beneath her wings. There's nothing you can do to make God love you any more than he already does, nothing you can do to cause her to love you any less.

God is love. If you can't grasp that, you can't grasp my gospel.

You have been taught that God loves you and those like you and will love others once they become like you or believe what you do, but this isn't unconditional love. That's an all-too-human love full of conditions and limitations. There's nothing divine or radical about that. I'm saying God is love—that God loves those you hate as much as she loves you. I'm saying God doesn't condemn anyone, doesn't punish anyone, doesn't reject anyone—only loves, only accepts, only gives, only waits, only cares for, only loves. Loves. Loves. Loves.

And what is this love? Absolute and unconditional acceptance. Compassion and passion. Giving and extending. No judgment. No condemnation. No expectation. No strings. No demands.

You've heard people condemn other people in my name. You've heard them say God condemns them. This is when my gospel is lost. This is when lies are called the truth.

That's it. God is love. And to be like God, to be my followers, is to love the way God loves—no conditions, no strings, no condemnation, no expectation, no sides, no tribes, no religions, no us and them, no reward and punishment.

If you accept this, you will trust. You will have peace. You will allow God's great love, which is God herself, to flow through you to others.

God will provide and care for you just like he does for the birds of the air and the flowers of the fields. Don't worry. Don't be selfish or greedy. Don't hoard your stuff. Share what you have with others. Give to those in need in the same way God gives to you. Truly trust God, and demonstrate that you do by giving, sharing, bearing one another's burdens.

Don't judge others. Be merciful. Be compassionate. Actually put yourself in the place of others and feel what it's like to be them. Feel what they feel. Care about their problems as much as you do your own. This makes you children of God—kind, gracious, giving.

If you trust God, actually believe she will take care of you, you can dare to live with freedom, hope, and abandon. You can be so secure that you relax and learn how to be yourself, stop fighting for your place or recognition, stop tearing others down in order to make yourself feel better.

God's reign is unlike anything you've ever experienced. The last are first, those that serve are greatest. To find your life, you have to lose it. To receive, you have to give.

Spend your time caring for others. God will care for you.

Give to those who ask of you. Share what you have. It all belongs to God anyway, and she has plenty. You don't need two coats if there's someone without one.

Love your enemies.

If someone hurts you, don't try to hurt them back. What would that accomplish? Be like God who loves everyone, who has mercy and compassion for everyone. Think of the opportunity you have to embody God by blessing those who curse you, praying for those who despise you.

Love those who don't love you. If you do, you will be like God, who lets his sun shine on the just and unjust, his rain fall on the good and the evil. If you only love those who love you, what have you done? Who doesn't do that? Love everyone—even those who hate you—and demonstrate your singular and certain conviction that God has enough love to go around.

Lucky are the unlucky. Rich are the poor. Blessed are the cursed. Happy are the mourners. Full are the hungry. Why? Because if you do what God wants you to, they will have all they need. You can feed and clothe and comfort them. You can care for those who can't care for themselves, defend the defenseless, heal the hurting, love the unlovable.

My gospel is the good news that God is love—news so surprising, so wildly wonderful and unexpected that it can turn your world upside down. In fact, if you not only hear and receive this gospel, but actually become it for others, it will turn their worlds upside down too.

In a Word

If there's one word that captures the teachings of Jesus, their core, his essence, it's *love*.

Both in what he taught and how he lived, Jesus embodied love. According to Jesus, God is love. It's not just what God does, but who and what God is.

God is love, and all God asks of us is love. Love God with all we have and love our neighbors as ourselves—do these and we've done all we need to do. A lot of people before Jesus and a lot of people after (even ones calling themselves by his name) have said there's a lot more to abundant, meaningful, God-pleasing life than that, but not Jesus. According to him, love is all.

Implicit in loving our neighbors as ourselves is our loving ourselves, not selfishness or narcissism, but a genuine acceptance and appreciation that can only come from the security and confidence that we are loved by God. When we know who we are, love and accept ourselves, then we are not an issue. It's only when people really aren't secure in who they are and the fact that they are loved and accepted that self-centeredness and narcissism, genuine self-love's perversions, occur.

If God is love, then sin is anything that prevents us from receiving God's love, loving ourselves, and loving others fully, completely, liberally. Sin is missing the mark. The mark is love.

To Jesus, religion is love—not morality or ethics (he showed how impossible true morality is by saying, You have heard of old do not kill, but I say unto you, anyone who hates his brother is a murderer…, etc.), not rules or rituals (he often violated the rules and rituals of his religion to the scandal of the religious leaders of his day), but compassion. Everywhere Jesus went, he was moved with compassion. Compassion means to feel what another person is feeling, to put ourselves in their place, travel for a while in their skin. Self-centeredness makes this impossible unless the person is very much like us.

Unfortunately, we have many parents, religious and political leaders, and celebrities who are so low on love themselves that they're not teaching it or demonstrating it to those they influence. They are wounded or have not been taught to love themselves.

The residual effects of Puritanism still linger. So many among us still believe that the approval (and love) of God comes only when we are pure or moral or holy or righteous. This is what the Puritans believed, what the Pharisees before them believed. Religious leaders who should be our teachers of love are more moralists than lovers. They use fear and guilt because they don't trust love. Love requires freedom, the ability to reject the love being offered. Love is dangerous. It's an act of faith. It's much easier to use fear, guilt, and manipulation.

When we limit God's love, it's because we're projecting our limitations onto God. We say God's love is unconditional, but we don't really believe it, don't really live like it. We say it, then in the next breath put all kinds of conditions on God's love. If we really knew it, had really experienced it, really taken it in and accepted it, we would relax and live with far more abandon, and we'd find it far more easy and comfortable to love others instead of judging and condemning them.

God is love. It is who and what God is and what God does— not based on anything we do or do not do. If we grow in God's love and become more loving people, God doesn't love us any more, just as if we stay selfish, ignorant, and hateful, God doesn't love us any less. God loves those who are most unlike us as much as she loves us.

A god who hates, who destroys, who punishes, who chooses sides is a human projection of fear onto an unknown, distant deity, but perfect love casts out fear.

God loves us. There's nothing we can do to earn, deserve, increase, or decrease that love.

If God is love, and if she who loves knows God and he who does not love does not know God, then God is present in every act of love, no matter how feeble or flawed, and absent from acts that are unloving and indifferent.

But what is love?

Love isn't just a feeling, because feelings come and go. Love is a lifestyle, a commitment, a way of being in the world, a choice, a type of religion, and a political stance. Love is an action (not just an expression). Love is extending ourselves on behalf of and in the service of what's best for others (what they really need). Love is meeting another's need. If we see someone who is hungry, love is feeding them. If we see someone who is lonely, love is visiting with them. If we see someone hurting someone else, love is stopping them. In its purest sense, love is meeting someone's need who can't do anything for us in return.

Who doesn't love those who love them? Jesus asks. Who doesn't loan money to those who can pay them back? Pure love does for those who can't do for themselves and who can't do for us, who couldn't possibly pay us back. Love is the antithesis of selfishness.

Love is not like. We can love people without particularly liking them. Love is a commitment to doing what's best for others whether we like their attitude or politics or personality or nationality or sexuality or morality or not. Our ability to love someone has everything to do with what's inside us and nothing to do with the person we're loving. It's not contingent on whether they are lovable, but on how much capacity to love we have.

It's what we most yearn for, what we, and those around us, most need.

Everything I believe in and hope for is, in a word, love.

Acknowledgements

For support and encouragement and invaluable contributions:

Adam Ake, Jennifer Jones, Lynn Wallace, David Lister, John Bridges, Thomas Moore, Marcus Borg, Frederick Buenchner, Andrew Greeley, Jill Mueller, Bette Powell, Fran Oppenheimer, Amy Moore-Benson, Jason Hedden, Emily Balazs, Ben Leroy, Michael Connelly, Van Willis, Mike and Judi Lister, Tony Simmons, River Jordan, Ansley Henkel, Jeff Moore, Dave Lloyd, LaDonna Paulk, Randy Renfroe, Tricia Weeks, Betty Holloway, Cedric Lenox, Jan Waddy, Pam and Micah and Meleah Lister, Travis Roberson, and Harley Walsh.

For further reading, I highly recommend:
(these books even include biblical references and notes :-))

The Jesus I Never Knew by Philip Yancey
The Essential Jesus by John Dominic Crossan
A Marginal Jew by John P. Meier
Who Killed Jesus by John Dominic Crossan
Meeting Jesus Again for the First Time by Marcus J. Borg
The Hidden Jesus by Donald Spoto
What Jesus Meant by Gary Wills
Christ by Jack Miles
The Meaning of Jesus by Marcus J. Borg and N.T. Wright
The Real Jesus by Luke Timothy Johnson
Scribbling in the Sand by Thomas Moore
Saving Jesus from the Church by Robin R. Meyers
The Gospel of Jesus by James M. Robinson
Jesus: A Life by A.N. Wilson
The Gospel According to Jesus by Stephen Mitchell
Desire of the Everlasting Hills by Thomas Cahill
The Gospel of Thomas by Marvin Meyer
Gnostic Gospels by Elaine Pagels

Michael Lister

A native Floridian, award-winning novelist, Michael Lister grew up in North Florida near the Gulf of Mexico and the Apalachicola River where most of his books are set.

In the early 90s, Lister became the youngest chaplain within the Florida Department of Corrections—a unique experience that led to his critically acclaimed mystery series featuring prison chaplain John Jordan: POWER IN THE BLOOD, BLOOD OF THE LAMB, FLESH AND BLOOD, THE BODY AND THE BLOOD, and BLOOD SACRIFICE.

Michael won a Florida Book Award for his literary thriller, DOUBLE EXPOSURE, a book, according to the *Panama City News Herald*, that "is lyrical and literary, written in a sparse but evocative prose reminiscent of Cormac McCarthy." His other thrillers include THUNDER BEACH, BUNRT OFFERINGS, and SEPARATION ANXIETY.

Michael also writes a popular weekly column on art and meaning and life titled *Of Font and Film* (www.OfFontandFilm.com), which includes reviews of film and fiction. A collection of these has been published titled THE MEANING OF LIFE IN MOVIES.

His website is www.MichaelLister.com.

THE MEANING OF LIFE IN MOVIES

"A Rashomon ride! Michael Lister's perceptions of film and the life it captures are guaranteed to be unique and intriguing. Read this book! You won't be disappointed."
Michael Connelly

MICHAEL LISTER

AUTHOR OF DOUBLE EXPOSURE

CPSIA information can be obtained at www.ICGtesting.com
Printed in the USA
LVOW071537121111

254487LV00007B/1/P